RISKY FAITH

Becoming **BRAVE ENOUGH**
to **TRUST THE GOD**
who is **BIGGER** than your world

To Dottie
Blessings!
Susan Yates

RISKY FAITH

Becoming **BRAVE ENOUGH**
to **TRUST THE GOD**
who is **BIGGER** than your world

SUSAN ALEXANDER YATES

LOYAL
ARTS MEDIA

Published by
Loyal Arts Media
P.O. Box 1414
Bend, OR 97709
loyalartsmedia.com

Printed in the United States of America

Cover design by Jessica Blanchard
Author photo by Katarina Price Photography

ISBN 978-1-929125-45-6 (paperback)

What Others Are Saying About Risky Faith

"The truest learning, the deepest learning, is always over-the-shoulder and through-the-heart. In her new book, Susan Yates invites us to come along with her as she lives, like all of us, in this very now-but-not-yet world, one where some things are clear and much is not, where we know some things with certainty, and where we live with perplexity too. With the hard-won wisdom of years, she reflects on the God she knows and the people she knows, twining them together in a thoughtfully winsome account of the questions and answers that are at the heart of everyone's life. *Risky Faith* will be a trusted guide for those who long to understand the depth and breadth of apprenticing oneself to the God who is at one and the same time our Father and in heaven, who is both merciful and mighty—simply said, the God of honest and historic faith."

~ **Dr. Steven Garber**, author of
Visions of Vocation: Common Grace for the Common Good, and principal at
the Washington Institute for Faith, Vocation & Culture
and **Meg Garber**, Elementary School Librarian,
Falls Church, Virginia

"Nothing in all life is easier and harder, simpler but more profound than trusting God. Gently, wisely, strongly and helpfully, Susan Yates shows us how and brings us back to what we all know but need to know again, and again, and again."

~ **Os and Jenny Guinness,**
authors of many books including *The Call*

"We focus too much on the bigness of our problems and too little on the greatness of our God. Susan's book changes all that by challenging readers to take a fresh look at the awesome God they serve."

~ **Matthew L. Jacobson**, MatthewLJacobson.com

"So many of us walk around weighed down by a strong sense of heaviness. We can feel overwhelmed by the challenging situations and difficult relationships that we find ourselves in. We're left wondering where to turn and how we can live richer and fuller lives. It's this very thing that I love about *Risky Faith*—Susan Yates has an unusual ability to take deep truths from the Word of God and apply them to our real life problems. Her book isn't merely 'fascinating' or 'thought-provoking'—although it is both of these—its message has the power to be life-changing."

~ **Lisa Jacobson**, Club31Women.com

"Practical atheist! We've all been there when it's time to put our money where our mouth is. Susan Yates walks us through her own experience with conviction and compassion. She reminds us what we already know, but somehow have forgotten, so that the next time our faith is put to the test, we can remember that God is indeed big enough!"

~ **Dr. Tim and Darcy Kimmel**,
Speakers and authors of *Grace Based Parenting* and
Grace Filled Marriage

"As a woman, wife, and mother, I am grateful for the wisdom of Susan Yates. Her words are practical yet powerful. *Risky Faith* is gently wrapped around God's truth and purposefully draws you, as a reader, into the reality of His presence."

~ **Wynter Pitts**,
Author and Founder "For Girls Like You" Magazine and Devotional

"Susan's book touches on important issues for every believer, but especially for those who grapple with fear and have trouble trusting God in the everyday and big issues of life. She encourages us to know who God is, and to REMEMBER who He is. She reminds us that we need a bigger vision of a greater God."

~ **Bob and Mary Ann Lepine**, Family Life Today

"Reading Susan Yates delightful book *Risky Faith*, brought to mind what Christian author A. W. Tozer once said: 'What comes into our minds when we think about God is the most important thing about us.' Yates insightfully addresses the things that keep us from seeing God accurately and what enables us to understand and worship God with greater clarity. Her book is full of godly wisdom that evidences years of experience in applying God's truth to everyday life. I recommend it highly!"

~ **Rebecca Manley Pippert,**
author of *Out of the Salt Shaker* and *Live/Grow/Know*

"I have deep admiration for Susan Yates and her ministry to women across the country. Growing up in a pastor's home I know the rare faithfulness that's required of a longtime pastor's wife, mother, grandmother, not to mention author and speaker. Susan has experience, wisdom, and knows her Bible. I highly recommend the encouragement you'll receive from answering the question she's posed to us in this book, *Risky Faith.*"

~ **Kelly Minter,**
Bible teacher and LifeWay Bible study author

"The simplest and most essential truths of the Christian faith are the ones we need to hear repeatedly, day after day, else we are apt to forget them. Susan Yates recognizes this and has done a great service in *Risky Faith*, reminding us that no matter how awful our problems and fears seem, God is bigger than all of them. Accessible yet profound, this book will be a reassurance and comfort to all who read it."

~ **Art Lindsley,**
Ph.D. Vice President of Theological Initiatives Institute for Faith, Work & Economics,
Author of *C. S. Lewis's Case for Christ*
and **Connie Lindsley,**
Partner, Oasis Discipleship and Teaching ministry

"With years of ministry, fourteen books, and twenty-one grandchildren to her credit, you'd think Susan Yates would have no problem trusting God. And yet she sometimes wonders if He is loving enough, powerful enough, or BIG ENOUGH to handle it all. 'I need a bigger vision of our great God,' she says. Don't we all? Part memoir, part how-to book, *Risky Faith* is a candid invitation to push the limits, expand your perspective, and discover just how great God really is."

~ **Jodie Berndt,**
author of *Praying the Scriptures for Your Children*,
The Undertaker's Wife, and other books

"For women who are single, married, in the throes of childrearing, or the transition of an empty nest, Susan Yates' *Risky Faith* offers practical insight and advice, spiritual comfort and conviction, and gracious wisdom for the ages."

~ **Amy Julia Becker,**
author of *Small Talk* and *A Good and Perfect Gift*

"This book will give you the chance to dig deep and examine the most important thing in your life—what you think about when you think about your heavenly Father. *Risky Faith* will encourage, strengthen, and help you to discover how awesome your God truly is. Susan Yates is a compelling writer, which you're about to discover. I highly recommend this book to you."

~ **Dr. Robert Wolgemuth,** best-selling author

"Yes, our God IS big enough! Susan Yates opens our eyes and hearts to understand that He is bigger than anything that concerns us!"

~ **Archbishop Foley and Allison Beach,**
Anglican Church of North America

"As an ophthalmologist, I spend the majority of my day helping people optimize their vision. I employ every step necessary—glasses, contacts, medications, or surgery to help them in this endeavor. When I am successful, people enjoy vision with clarity, depth, field, and color to its full potential. What an illustration of the way the Holy Spirit helps us optimize our ability to see God, taking us from darkness into the light. When this is fully realized, we will see Him as He really is and ourselves as we really are. In this book, Susan Yates diagnoses many of the ailments that prevent our seeing our God in all His love, power, and sovereignty. In her gentle wisdom, she offers steps we can all take on this journey of a lifetime."

~ Jessica Oliver, MD

"Finally! A book that covers all the basics of spiritual life by addressing the questions and felt needs of people just like you and me. I am so grateful for the wisdom and authenticity of Susan Alexander Yates as she walks the reader through her lifetime of seeking a fresh vision of God in her new book *Risky Faith*. Whether addressing issues such as sin and the enemy or sharing one of the many illustrative anecdotes from her own journey, Yates' ultimate aim is to help us peel back the layers and see God as One who is far bigger than we ever imagined. My favorite part was the juxtaposition of natural growth versus spiritual growth and the opportunity for reflection and further study at the end of each chapter. Thank you, Susan, for this invaluable primer on how to see God clearly in our risky and rewarding life of faith. I cannot wait to recommend this to others."

~ **Lucinda Secrest McDowell**, author *Dwelling Places*

DEDICATION

Lovingly dedicated to my grandchildren:

Caroline Alexander Gaskins, William Steve Gaskins,
John Tucker Gaskins, Graham Scott Gaskins,
David Yates Gaskins, Sylvia Tucker Yates,
Isabel Grey Yates, John William Yates IV,
Joseph Alexander Yates, Tobin Powers Yates,
Cashel Dean Yates, Linden Leah Yates,
Saylor Frances Yates, Blaine Scott Anderson,
Hayes Christopher Anderson, Sloan Yates Anderson,
Greyson Alexander Wilson, Mimi Sullivan Wilson,
McLean Caruthers Wilson, Yates Kemmons Wilson,
Tucker FitzSimons Wilson

Sweet ones, here's a prayer that I pray regularly
for each one of you:

"I do not cease to give thanks for you,
remembering you in my prayers,
that the God of our Lord Jesus Christ, the Father of glory,
may give you a spirit of wisdom and of revelation in the
knowledge of him, having the eyes of your
hearts enlightened, that you may know
what is the **hope** to which he has called you,
what are the **riches** of his glorious inheritance in the saints,
and what is the immeasurable greatness of his **power**
toward us who believe."
~ Ephesians 1:17-19 (emphasis mine)

Table of Contents

INTRODUCTION

I was absolutely miserable. Stuck in a middle seat on a packed international flight, I could barely move my arms or legs. The air was stifling. Next to me a man snored shamelessly, his mouth opening and shutting in concentrated rhythm. Like a yo-yo on a string, drool hanging from his chin.

I was dirty, smelly, and my back ached. My body felt like it was encased in a straight jacket. And I still had hours and hours to go.

For several weeks my husband John and I had been speaking in Africa. It had been a tremendous time but now my body was shutting down. I felt like my adrenaline was leaking from every pore. I was exhausted mentally, physically, emotionally, and spiritually.

As I sat in my tight bundle I began to think about my children. I missed them and couldn't wait to get my two feet on the same continent as theirs. All five were adults now, out of the nest and making their ways through college and jobs. Turning my thoughts to them, I focused on one in particular. I had a sense of uneasiness about this specific child. How was this child really doing? Was there a problem that needed attention? What if there were? Suppose this child was in real trouble? What if things were worse than I thought? As I continued to think and worry about the child, the possible problem began to grow in my imagination. The more I considered my child, the more anxious I became. Soon my stomach was in knots. I felt claustrophobic.

This is ridiculous, I said to myself. *I'll get out my Bible and read. Surely that will help.* It did not help. *Okay, I need to pray so that's what I'll do.* That did not help either. More anxious and discouraged than before, I sat in a fearful paralysis. Finally I uttered a prayer of just three words, a prayer that was to change everything. "Help me, Lord."

The answer that came was not audible but it was abundantly clear and unmistakably from Him. Two simple words: "*Remember Me.*" So simple, so profound, and exactly what I needed at that moment.

With the stress of this smothering flight, I had let my concern for this child grow and grow. It had become so big in my head that the problem itself became my focus. Perspective was lost. Instead I was overwhelmed by this current issue.

I finally realized **I had forgotten who God was.** I had forgotten how very much He loved my child and me. I had forgotten He knew my child much better than I did. I had forgotten He was working in ways I could not see. He was in this issue, totally involved, and His love was perfect. He was so much bigger than I gave Him credit for. It wasn't that these concepts were new to me. It was more that I wasn't living day in and day out in the assurance and knowledge of how BIG He is. I was missing out, and the result was anxiety, loss of perspective, and an anemic understanding of God's personal love.

So why this book?

I need it. I really need it.

Perhaps you do too.

CHAPTER ONE

WHEN OUR ISSUES BECOME BIGGER THAN OUR GOD

Hearing God speak to me on that crowded airplane was a turning point in my life. In His words, *"Remember Me,"* lay a gentle, yet strangely comforting rebuke.

I realized my imagination had run wild. I had allowed my concern for my child to become bigger than my God. I had forgotten who He was. And He wanted me to remember.

In thinking about this experience for many years, I have realized that no matter what season of life I am in, there is usually at least one big concern uppermost on my mind. It might be a strong-willed toddler who is about to break me. Or a teenager who keeps me up worrying at night. Perhaps it's a relationship that has become very painful—a friend who just doesn't understand or a family member who is estranged. For some it might be the longing for a mate, wondering: *Will I ever find the right person?* You may be suffering from the ongoing pain of infertility or a marriage in crisis. Perhaps you have a hole in your life because you are an empty nester. Your job may be at risk or you or your spouse may not be able to find work.

Finances, or rather the lack of them, may be your constant headache. Perhaps you are in a job you intensely dislike. You may feel anxious because you don't know what career to pursue. The serious illness of a family member or a close friend may be causing a deep sadness. It may just be the overwhelming stresses of living in the twenty first century that cause havoc in our lives. Stress, anxiety, pressure, worry, and fear have become all too familiar.

The truth is we all have issues. It's a part of living in this world. A wise person once said, "Life wouldn't be so hard if we hadn't expected it to be so easy."

When I'm really honest with myself I realize that much of the time I let my issue of the moment become bigger than my God. It just seems to grow and grow in my mind. It controls my disposition. My concern easily expands while my view of God slowly fades. And then I become stressed or anxious feeling like it's all up to me. And I lose perspective.

As a believer in God the Father, His Son Jesus, and the power of His Holy Spirit, I know God doesn't want me to live like this. He loves me and you with a perfect Father's love. He wants us to trust Him with everything. That sounds really simple, but it is oh so hard!

WHY IS IT SO HARD TO TRUST?

It's really hard to trust someone you don't know. This is true in personal relationships. When I first became acquainted with my future husband John, I didn't know him. I knew others who knew him and thought well of him. In fact I remember asking Larry, a mutual friend, if John was someone you could count on. He looked good, he sounded good, but what was he really like?

During our last two years of college we got to know each other well. No, we didn't date. Both of us were going out with other people. But he became my close friend. There is something special about a best friend of the opposite sex who you are not interested in and who is not interested in you. You don't have to play games. They are safe. You don't have to worry about what you say or do because there's no risk of breaking up. He was after all just my best friend. Over time I got to know him better. I watched how he interacted with others. I saw him in different situations. Spending time with his family gave me insights into his character as I got to know those who had shaped him. Asking him questions, seeing him struggle with tough issues, and hearing his dreams all added to my knowledge of this man. After three years of being just best friends, John finally saw the light. (my version of course!). Three months later we were married. Did marriage mean that I completely knew this man? Of course not. I had a basic confidence in who he was and a deep desire to spend the rest of my life getting to know him. Forty-six years later I am still discovering the depths of this amazing man. Marriage would be boring if the growth and discoveries (and even hard times) were over once we said, "I do."

Just as any relationship begins at the acquaintance level, so does our relationship with God. Our knowledge is shaped by what others say, by what we read, observe, and hear, and by our personal experiences.

Some of us have known Him for a long time, others are

just getting acquainted with Him, and perhaps some are waiting to be introduced to Him. No matter what our relationship level with God is we all have one thing in common: we would like to be able to trust Him. The better we know Him the easier it is to trust Him but so often we get overwhelmed with an issue in our life and soon our issue becomes bigger than our God. Even when we know Him we can still have the tendency to withdraw from Him or forget Him. It comes in a variety of ways:

We run from Him.

Life gets tough. A situation arises. We may consider Him for a moment but then thoughts creep in, *I got myself into this situation, I can't help myself, I don't know how to help my child …* We blame ourselves. We beat ourselves up once again for our pasts. In our shame we begin to run from Him. Like the apostle Peter we may even *deny* him.

We are afraid of Him.

Sometimes we are afraid of Him. He is so big and so good and we are not. We fear we'll let Him down. (We will.) We fear He will withdraw His love. (He won't.) We fear He isn't really in control. (He is.) We fear what we can't totally know or control.

We ignore Him.

Often in ignoring Him we take on the responsibility of thinking, *I should be able to handle this myself.* This is easy for us moms. We are good problem solvers. We have to be. Our nurturing instincts necessitate problem solving. Perhaps you oversee a team in your company. A tough situation arises. Personality conflict rears its ugly head. Office morale dips to a new low. And so we put on our fix-it hats and proceed to fix everyone around us—our girl friends, our employees, our husbands, our children, even ourselves. We may make some progress but the reality is we can't fix everything or everyone. We get frustrated. We fail. Finally we realize we are ignoring Him.

Some choose to ignore Him because they don't really believe in an all-powerful God who loves them intensely or who is interested in them intimately. Or a God who is sovereignly in control of all things.

Others fall prey to cultural pressure that ridicules anyone who might believe. Instead of lovingly engaging a critic, our courage falters and we remain silent, ignoring the power of the gospel within us.

Often we ignore Him because we are afraid He won't come through for us. And we don't want to find that out. That would be scary.

We try to figure Him out.

I am very good at this. I assume that if X happens then God is saying one thing. Otherwise He means Y. I determine how I think He should work and when. And I don't even realize it. The reality is I'm dictating to God how to be God! I'm putting Him in a box. I am severely limiting who I believe Him to be. When I'm brutally honest I recognize my real problem is that I just want to be God. Or I'd like to try to manage Him. At some level any way. It's laughable isn't it: "I, Susan, want to manage God!"

If we peel back the layers of all our efforts, of our own self-protection, we realize again we are not enough. At our core, each of us wants and needs something more, something bigger than ourselves.

WHAT WE REALLY WANT

I suspect what we really want is to believe in a power bigger and stronger than ourselves. We long to know there is one person who understands us. One who is ultimately in charge and is perfectly capable of handling all things.

What we really need is a greater understanding and deeper experience of just how big God is. The eminent French mathematician and philosopher Blaise Pascal said, "There is a God-shaped vacuum in the heart of every man which cannot be filled by any created thing but by God himself made known through Jesus Christ. "

We want to accept God's perfect personal love for us—a love not based on our behavior but on His character. He cannot help loving us. It is His nature, His number one character trait, His top priority. It's far easier to believe this in our heads than in our hearts. We know our hearts are not pure. We struggle because what we want collides with what we experience.

BELIEVING IS A PROCESS

Just as getting to know a person is a process, so is getting to know God. It is not instant. I didn't instantly know my husband John. I am still in process. The more time I spend with him the better I know him. This is true in any relationship. We get to know someone when we spend time with him or her. Some relationships will turn into deep friendships and others will disappoint or dissolve.

But a relationship with God will not disappoint. This

doesn't mean we will understand how or why He does what He does. Like David we will get angry with Him, like Jonah we may hide from Him, like Job we may feel hurt by Him. But He will, as He has for these men and countless others, convince us of His perfect love for us. It isn't likely to happen all at once but He will do it as we spend time getting to know Him.

J. B. Phillips, an Anglican writer and Bible translator, wrote a popular book in 1955 called *Your God Is Too Small.*[1] What he meant by this is that our *view* of God is too small. God isn't small but our characterization of Him is. He is so much bigger than we think. Phillips was right. My view of God is too small and I imagine yours is too. But what if we could catch a glimpse of how much bigger He is? If we could, I suspect we'd become more confident of the personal, unconditional love He has for you and for me.

I'd like to say I've learned how big God is and am convinced of His perfect love for my children and me. I'd like to say I no longer struggle with issues. But it's simply not true. The truth is I still struggle, but now I realize the real key is that I need a bigger vision of our great God. I need for my understanding of His power and love to grow. I desperately want to really believe He is all-powerful and all loving. I realize it is only as my view of Him increases daily in my head that I will be more able to view my issues with a proper perspective. Is there a quick way to do this? No. It's a lifetime journey—a path with lots of setbacks but many encouragements along the way.

This book isn't a three-step formula to completely understanding how big God is. It won't enable you or me to accept once and for all the absolute assurance of His perfect love. It won't completely cure worry and anxiety. Converting head knowledge into real living is a fluid process with ups and downs and it takes time. However you will discover some insights that will enable you to experience a greater assurance of how big He is and yet how intimately involved He desires to be in your life.

Life is full of risks. As we acknowledge and accept the earthly risks associated with trusting and following Jesus in all of the issues of life, we will more deeply understand the need for the eyes of our hearts to be opened to behold our great God.

Outside my window is a Japonica bush. At the moment its tiny pink flowers are closed up in tight buds. We've had a record cold winter so these buds have been delayed in opening up. Even now, a chilly western wind is blowing and last night's unusually late frost is dissipating. The little buds seem stuck but I know that beneath what I can see, growth is occurring. Underneath the soil, moisture is enabling the roots to nourish the branches in ways I can't see or imagine.

God is so much bigger than we can see or imagine. And most amazing of all, He longs for us to know Him at a much greater depth. Just like my Japonica bush, God has been at work in your life and in mine, preparing the soil in order that we might know Him more fully and experience His bigness in fresh new ways. He will cause us to blossom.

A TIME TO REFLECT

1. What issue is consuming your thoughts? Has this issue grown in your head to the place where it overshadows the presence and power of God?
2. List any fears you have about giving your issue to God.
3. What would you like for God to do in your life?
4. If you were to hear God say, "(your name), I cannot help loving you," how would you respond?

FOR FURTHER STUDY:

Read Ephesians chapter one (This is a letter written by the apostle Paul about A.D. 60 to his friends in the city of Ephesus, one of the most famous cities of that day in Asia. Paul, formerly a violent man whose mission was to destroy the church, has become a believer and writes this from a prison cell in Rome.)

1. Underline each description of Jesus or God.
2. Circle everything They have done or do for you.
3. What specific things does Paul pray for his friends in verses 15-23? What three things does he want you to know?

You might pray these verses of prayer for yourself as you read this book.

"I do not cease to give thanks for you, remembering you in my prayers, that the God of our Lord Jesus Christ, the Father of glory, may give you a spirit of wisdom, and of revelation in the knowledge of him, having the eyes of your hearts enlightened, that you may know what is the **hope** to which he has called you, what are the **riches** of his glorious inheritance in the saints, and what is the immeasurable **greatness** of his power toward us who believe..." (Ephesians 1:16-19, emphasis mine).

CHAPTER TWO

TRUSTING GOD CAN BE RISKY

There were tears, buckets of tears. But also times when her eyes were dry because her heart was too numbed to produce any more tears.

My friend Jane had just been told her husband had been unfaithful not once but many, many times, going back years before and continuing throughout their marriage. It made no sense. He was a believer; she was a believer with a lifetime of Christian ministry. Others looked to them as the perfect family. They had fun together, he treated her well, and they had a great relationship with their kids.

But it was all a lie.

Devastated, she could only watch as his employers arranged for him to be sent to a treatment center. He was to be gone for three and a half months, spending time in two different centers. Hardest of all, she was not able to tell anyone. Because he traveled in his profession, his absence wasn't that unusual to their friends. But the devastation for her kids was almost too much for her to bear. The loneliness of her pain was brutal. The shock of betrayal was agony. For her whole life she had sought the Lord, taught in seminaries, and truly tried to please her Savior in every way. She had been a good girl. And now this. "How, oh Lord? Why, oh Lord? My children ..."

Would she ever be able to trust her husband again? It was a huge risk for her and there was no guarantee as to what the outcome would be.

But even more important, would she be able to trust God again? This would become the biggest risk of her life.

Most of us will not face such a huge risk as my friend has. Yet each of us will encounter risks that are scary, some that are good, and some that could completely alter our lives forever.

Taking a risk is a natural part of life.

All of our lives we will face risks—risks in relationships, in careers, in parenting, in faith, in making wise decisions. In a certain sense, the resume of our lives is a portfolio of risks. Some risks are good risks and others are foolish, even dangerous, or possibly life threatening. We may experience risks over which we have no control. Some will be big risks while others may seem small. In an increasingly technological world we are overwhelmed with options. The more options, the more risks. Options that will continue to increase for our children and grandchildren.

Each of us has a different capacity for risk taking.

Some of us are more natural risk takers and some of us are more cautious. Neither is better. We are merely different and each tendency has both negative and positive aspects.

A *natural risk taker* may be a visionary. This person probably has a sense of adventure and is quick and decisive. He is likely a person who gets an adrenalin rush from taking a risk. The down side of his personality is that he may not count the cost of the risk. He may fail to carefully weigh the options or to seek wise counsel from others. A *cautious risk taker* on the other hand might be a thoughtful person, carefully considering all sides of the risk, and less likely to make a fast decision that turns into a poor decision. The down side for this person is the paralysis of fear, which could lead to inaction.

It is important to remember that something that would be an easy risk for us may be very difficult for a friend. On the other hand, something easy for them might be an area in which we struggle. God made us unique and in our differences we have to choose compassion over criticism, support over withdrawal.

DIFFERENT TYPES OF RISKS

Our whole life is really a series of risks. As parents we teach our kids to take risks. It starts with their very first wobbly step. It's scary for the child yet we clap and we cheer her forward. We are there to catch her when she falls. We pick her up and urge her on. We know one little fall won't hurt. It's normal and she needs to get back up so she knows she can. It will not be long before one risky step has produced a feisty runner.

As our kids grow up the risks become more costly. Ask any parent who has just taken her child to get her driver's license, or a dad who has just given a young man permission to marry his only daughter. We have to let our children go. We want our kids to become independent but this is painfully risky for us parents. In today's child-oriented culture it is very easy to over parent—to protect and supervise them because we love them. Yet over-parenting (known as "helicopter parenting") will handicap your children and make them unable to take healthy risks. Your un-intended message to your child is "You can't do this so I will do it (make the decision, find the job, etc.) for you." This will cause your child to become insecure not secure[1]. Therefore we encourage our kids to take healthy risks—to run for an office they might not win, to go out for a team they may not make. Yes they will fail and we will be there to help them learn how to accept failure and rejection. It may be devastating to them but we know that taking a risk that doesn't turn out as we want it to is not likely to ruin their lives. Instead it is going to prepare them for real life. Why? Grown up life will have plenty of risks that lead not to success, but to failure. If we don't teach our children how to take risks and fail while they are young, how will they know how to do this as adults? Because we are older we have perspective. Looking back we see the losses in our own lives through a different set of lenses. And we see the growth that occurred. We have greater wisdom than our children do.

In the same way God has a bigger picture of your life and mine. His perspective is so much larger. It does pain him to see us suffer but He has promised to be with us in our suffering and to use all things, even failure, for good for those who love Him (Romans 8:28).

Taking a risk is a common fact of life for every person in the world, regardless of age or personality. Learning to step out and take a small risk will equip us and our kids for the bigger risks we will face in our lives. Volumes could be written on this topic but for now let's think in terms of personal and relational risk taking.

PERSONAL RISK TAKING

Even a risk, which appears primarily personal, will inevitably impact others because we do not live in isolation. We live in relationships. Here are several stories of personal risk-taking to encourage us and to challenge us.

A risky new job

Be willing to go out on a limb with Me. If I am leading you, it is the safest place to be. Your desire to live a risk-free life is a form of unbelief. Your longing to live close to Me is at odds with your attempts to minimize risk. You are approaching a crossroads in your journey. In order to follow Me wholeheartedly, you must relinquish your tendency to play it safe.[2]

This is the devotional entry my friend Martha read on the day she and her husband decided to purchase a new business. Her husband really wanted to do this. She, on the other hand, was terrified. They prayed, sought advice from others, and ultimately she felt that in their case she needed to let him do this and support him, even though she did not want to. She was by nature risk-adverse when it came to finances. She felt safer when she was in control. And this purchase was clearly a big risk with no guarantees of success. As she relates,

> Taking a risk can expose the idols in our lives. It shows us what or who we are putting our security in and challenges us to let go of that idol. I had to ask myself, "What am I so afraid of losing that it paralyzes me?" I realized it was my idols of financial stability and of control. I had to make a choice and I could not make the choice out of fear. It wasn't comfortable but we are not necessarily supposed to be comfortable. We are supposed to be obedient to what we think God is calling us to while asking Him to shut doors where He wishes. In a humorous sort of way I sensed God saying to me, "Did you really mean it when you said you'd follow Me?" I realized I meant it if it led to good things.

Two long hard years later still in debt, they continue to struggle in the business not knowing the eventual outcome. However God has used this journey to do amazing things in their marriage and in their lives individually. God has had a much greater agenda than merely the success or failure of a business.

The risk of choosing to love again

Suzanne's first marriage had ended in a nasty divorce. Her husband had deserted her and their four small children. Years had gone by and much healing had taken place in Suzanne's life. Yet her fear of abandonment still remained. Now another man had come into her life. A kind, gentle, stable, God- fearing man. As their friendship grew she felt her heart awaken with feelings of love. However these feelings led to fear. Could she trust her gut? After all her gut had misled her in the past. In order to survive she had become adept in exercising very tight control over her emotions. Was she willing to give her heart away again? It was a huge risk. A risk fraught with fears of all kinds. This wise man gave her plenty of time. He did not push her. Instead, he set about growing in his own faith and he waited. In time, God revealed to Suzanne that this risk was one she should take. He was in it. Now, ten years later, these two are devoted to one another, serving Christ in a variety of ways together. Whenever I see them I am overwhelmed by this visible sign of God's grace and redemption.

The risk of a big move

Judy couldn't believe she was even thinking about a move. She had a great job teaching, lots of friends, and no prevailing reason to leave her comfortable life. And yet there was restlessness within her to spread her wings and take a risk. Being single gave her the freedom to consider such a big change. But her mom was opposed. She simply did not understand why someone in her late twenties would want to do this. Yet Judy wondered, *When I get to be in my eighties and look back will I regret that I didn't take this risk?* Judy had a love for writing, for music, and for sitcoms. After much thought, prayer, and consultation with friends, she packed her bags and hopped in her old orange Plymouth to begin a road trip from Virginia to Hollywood, California. With no money, no job, and no housing she was off on a risky adventure. She did odd jobs, traded housing for work, took classes at four different schools in writing, and worked with well-known musical artists. Yes, it was hand to mouth but she felt protected by God. Even though she didn't make it big she has never felt this adventure was a waste. After three years, she returned to Virginia and to teaching, rich with stories and aware that in those three short years she had gained ten years of life experience. Even more important, she had learned to rely on God for her most basic needs. For her it was a risk worth taking.

A risky leap of faith

My friend Elizabeth grew up in an ethnically religious home, long on rules but short on grace. So by the time she got to college she had actively rejected Christianity. After reading Nietzsche and other philosophers she came to believe that Christianity was a kind of masochistic illness—everyone trying to be like Jesus though they knew they never would be. But as she says, "I was still left with the nagging question: If not Christianity, then what else?" After delving into a study of world religions, especially Buddhism and the Baha'i faith, participating in yoga retreats, and reading voraciously she began to create her own version of a cafeteria spirituality. Restless, anxious, and possessed by a constant need for approval, she achieved more and more at work by numbing her emotions with food (resulting in an eating disorder), addictive exercise, and alcohol, all while keeping a frenetic personal and professional schedule. By society's standards her life seemed picture perfect—brilliant mind, successful in her career, a great husband, world traveler, and eventually adorable kids. And yet she says, "My inner noise continued, my longing remained. And I just kept on going, seeking, driving harder, hoping that the emptiness, the fears, and the shame would someday, somehow just be melt away." A move took them to a new city where friends invited them to church. In an effort to expose their kids to religion, dutifully checking that box off their good parenting list, they decided to go. "I was blindsided by a sensation of being starved and getting a taste of something rich—by the music, the welcoming faces, and mostly by the teaching. And it happened Sunday after Sunday, a bit of something that looked ordinary but tasted gourmet." In her typical go for it manner, she began to study the Bible. At first she felt like an anthropologist, studying some strange subculture. A believing community surrounded her, accepted her questions, and loved her patiently while she searched for truth. Soon she found herself wanting to get closer to Jesus. It was for her a leap of faith, a risky letting go of control. God understood her and He met her in her wobbly, tentative step. As she recalls,

> One cold January morning as I was writing in my journal about something I had done wrong. I was blindsided by grace. It hit me with an internal force—Jesus died that I might be forgiven of this sin and of all my sins. He died the death I should have died. God no longer saw my sins. He counted them no more against me. I was truly made new. I was blindsided by a sensation of being starved and getting a taste of succulent food that satisfied like no earthly food ever did or could. I felt a rush

of gratitude, then amazement, a feeling of being accepted without having to do anything, a weight being lifted off my shoulders.

My smart, talented friend took a risk, a risk to believe—a leap of faith. And her leap landed her safely in the Savior's arms.

Relational risk taking

Taking a risk that involves others can be scary, really scary, because it is not just about me. It's about others as well. This risk you choose to take could have a significant impact on someone else. It could even backfire.

The risk of asking forgiveness

Marie and John had been invited to spend a cozy weekend away with friends in the mountains. It was winter, and John was eager for warm weather, not cold. Besides, they wanted to get away and spend time by themselves. They booked a last minute deal for a Florida weekend, and hoped they could sneak away unnoticed. Marie hadn't called to let her friends know they weren't coming because they didn't want to hurt their feelings. While walking to their gate at the airport, Marie and John saw another couple who were traveling to meet up with their mutual friends. "I knew I was busted, " said Marie and she immediately texted their hosts to say they weren't coming. "It was a little late. Deception was a bitter pill to swallow. I should have been honest from the beginning about how I felt but I wasn't. It felt like I had just slapped my friend right in the face." When Marie and John got home, they knew they had to go and ask their friends' forgiveness. They didn't know how they would be received, but it didn't really matter. It was the right thing to do. It was risky but they knew they had been wrong and before the Lord they had to be the ones to ask for forgiveness. They went not out of feeling, but out of obedience. "We need to apologize to you and to ask you to forgive us. We deceived you and should have told you our situation in the beginning. We know we have hurt you and we are deeply sorry. We have come to ask your forgiveness." After talking things through, their friends did forgive them. But, more significantly, their friends said, "What meant the most to us was that you would put yourself out and come to our house to apologize. That must have been so hard. Your doing that has impacted how we relate to each other as husband and wife and to others." This incident took their friendship to a deeper level than ever before. Confession and forgiveness turned sin into a blessing.

Helen and her girl friend had shared many things over the years—struggles, joys, and a common love for Christ. Yet lately Helen sensed her friend was in a hard place. She tried to offer advice to her, and it was not received well. In fact a tangible irritation developed in their relationship culminating in a hurtful email from her friend in which she criticized Helen, "You are trying to control my life and tell me what to do." Even though the criticism seemed unjustified, Helen knew she needed to apologize for whatever hurt she had caused. Perhaps she had been insensitive. Helen called her friend and apologized. Her apology was not well received. Her friend was still too wrapped up in anger. It seemed as if there was something else going on in her friend's life. But at this time there was nothing more for Helen to do except pray. She prayed for God to bless her friend and to bring reconciliation in his time. That's really all she knew to do.

Asking forgiveness is often risky. We don't want to do it and we don't know if it will be granted. I can't tell you how many times I've had to go to my husband or to my children or to a friend and say, "I shouldn't have said ..." or "I shouldn't have done ..." Most of the time I'd rather say, "But if you had ..." or "If you hadn't ..." We go to one another out of obedience, not because we feel like it. And we forgive another person out of obedience rather than our feelings. Feelings are real but they should not necessarily determine action. An immature person makes decisions based on his feelings whereas a mature person makes decisions based on what is right. It helps to recognize that forgiveness and trust are not synonymous. It takes time for feelings to be healed and trust to be restored. Often a very long time. However the healing cannot begin apart from forgiveness.

A risky intervention

My friend could see the writing on the wall. The increase in her husband's drinking was dramatic. He was behaving less and less like an adult, refusing to take any responsibility. In his stupors he would injure himself at home and refuse to go to the hospital for help. His disrespect of her and the kids was out of control. She was terrified when he drove the kids to their activities. Finally she faced her reality. She realized she was contributing to the problem by thinking it would go away. She had to stop denying it would get better. Instead she acknowledged the family was on a dangerous downhill path. As she wrestled with the truth, she knew the time had come for her to take action. She sought wise counsel and arranged for an intervention. Was this an easy step? No. The risk was great. She had no idea how he would respond. Would he agree to go for treatment or would he bolt? There was no way to know. With experienced counselors, she developed a plan for the intervention and for what she would do if it did not work. Having a plan was crucial. It helped her to calculate the risk. She knew she would have to live with whatever happened. And she knew that once she did this she would have to stick with the decisions. Of course she hoped and thought it would go well. Many friends gathered around her and prayed. The day for the intervention came. And it did not go well. He bolted. The pain that ensued was devastating and at times seemed unending. Yet my friend never regretted her decision. It was a risk she had to take for her own safety and the safety of her children.

The risk of telling the truth

A painful memory of my youth is still vivid in my head. I was about seven years old when my mom took my two younger brothers and me on a shopping spree to a stationery store. Wondering down the aisles I encountered rows and rows of pretty papers, bows, and knickknacks—all gloriously arranged to present a collage of beauty that should entice any buyer. For some reason I was particularly drawn to a large pack of colorful rubber bands. They were beautiful and I imagined shooting them at my brothers. Suspecting that my mom would not buy them for me, I carefully looked around to see if anyone would notice and then I simply put them in my pocket. On the way home from the store my mother, who did have eyes in the back of her head, asked me what was in my pocket. I must have been very busy in my pocket. "Nothing," I replied. My suspicious mother turned toward me and said, "Let me see." And of course she found the rubber bands. Immediately we got back in the car, returned to the store where I had to tell the manager what I had done, apologize, and return the rubber bands. To say I was humiliated was an understatement. The fact that I had stolen an item was wrong but the fact that I had lied to my mother was even more upsetting to her. I learned very quickly that I never wanted to steal anything again and that I did not want to lie either. Getting caught at a young age was a blessing. Doing something wrong and telling the truth about it is far less damaging than lying about what you have done. This is a double whammy. Truth telling is risky. It may hurt others and it will most likely have nasty consequences, but lying can quickly develop into a habit that numbs one's integrity until you come to the place where you believe your own lie. Telling the truth is a risk worth taking.[3]

WHY IS IT SO HARD TO TAKE A RISK?

Taking a risk does not come naturally. Emotions collide with courage. *I don't feel like taking this risk. It's out of my comfort zone. It is going to be painful. I can't guarantee the* outcome. *It might not end the way I want. I worry about the impact on others. I want to be in control.* And we second-guess ourselves.

We live in the Washington DC area. It is a city of risks, political risks. And every risk is weighed against potential results. Results that can be determined by one's standing in the polls. New York is a city of risks. Every day huge financial risks are taken on Wall Street. Profits or losses dictate results. Whether it is poll numbers or financial numbers, risks are evaluated by results. But is this always the right way to evaluate a risk? Not necessarily. Of course we have to weigh the consequences before taking a vote or intervening in the world's problems. We must calculate financial decisions carefully and make wise decisions based on possible outcomes of profit or loss. However it is easy to place results above doing what is right. Taking risks is hard because we cannot always control results or the response of others to our decisions. Our first priority is to be men and women of integrity, seeking God's will and doing what would be pleasing in His sight. And that might mean making a very unpopular decision in the eyes of man. It may lead not to success but to failure in the eyes of the world.

DOES TAKING A GOOD RISK LEAD TO SUCCESS?

No. It often leads to failure. In fact God may lead us to take a risk He knows will intentionally lead to failure. What? Why would God want us to fail? He sees life from a different perspective, a much greater perspective, and He's about something so much bigger than our one risk.

John the Baptist took a risk when he came out of the wilderness and preached repentance to crowds of Israelites. He was called by God to take this risk as a significant role in preparing for the coming of the Messiah. Did his obedience to God's call bring about success? Men and women of that day would say no. John's ministry resulted in his having his head chopped off and delivered on a plate to a raging King Herod at his own birthday party.

Jesus died on the cross. Such a familiar phrase. A successful ending? Not in the eyes of many in that day. Most likely His life would have been determined a failure. But God was about something so much bigger.

If God is leading us to take a risk there is no guarantee of the outcome. Contrary to what we so often hear preached and what the world tells us to expect, "God will not let us fail," we might just fail. The problem is we define failure our way. *God will certainly make me successful because I'm following Him*, we think. We tend to see our circumstances as validating our decision. God on the other hand values our obedience—period. He has a much bigger agenda than we do and if fulfilling His will results in worldly failure it is not failure to Him. Taking a risk may end in failure but if we involve God in our decision it always leads to a deeper intimacy with Him. He is far more interested in our relationship with Him than in our success in taking a risk. Intimacy with our heavenly Father trumps success.

In making wise decisions we need both wisdom and courage.

THE ROLE OF WISDOM:

When you ask the big question, "How do I know if this is a good risk, one that I should take?" four actions will be helpful.

Seek wisdom from God

If we want to make wise decisions we must spend time with God in prayer and in a study of His Word. God never leads contrary to His Word. Ask Him to close a door that is not right. You may not hear a rousing "Go for it" but "Take the next step," trusting He will intervene as He knows is best. If anything about the risk involves sin or lacks integrity, run. If it will draw you away from Christ, run. (We will look more at this in chapter five.)

Seek guidance from family and friends

Ask the advice of others who love Christ, who are people of integrity, and who know you well. These should be people who push you toward a greater obedience to Christ. Listen to their perspectives even if it is not what you want to hear. Ask those who know you well, "Where have you seen God use me?" "What gifts and weaknesses do you see in me?" "Is there anything about this decision that I should consider that I might not have thought of?"

Seek good resources

There are many good books on the subject of calling. *The Call* by Os Guinness, *Kingdom Calling* by Amy Sherman, and *Visions of Vocation* by Steven Garber are three of our favorites. There are also many personal inventories and gift assessment tools on the Internet that can be of invaluable help.

Seek healing as needed

One of the fastest growing ministries in our church is our healing ministry. Most of us need healing in some area; we are all broken. Many need physical healing, others emotional healing. Some long to have the chains of family dysfunction broken in order to become the first of a new generation of healthy families. It can be risky to seek healing. After all, there are a lot of quacks out there. What if we pray for healing or have someone pray over us and it doesn't work? What will that do to our faith, our child's faith? Lots of questions with no simple answers. It may seem easier to remain with unresolved pain. However this unresolved issue can cloud our vision of God. Our brokenness influences the paradigm in which we understand and experience God. When we open ourselves to healing we open ourselves to a deeper and truer experience of God. We will see Him through a new set of lenses rather than a distorted pair. A prayer for healing is a risky option but it is a good risk—one we want to take.

My friend Laurie grew up in a home where she experienced regular emotional and verbal abuse from her mother. No matter what she did she never felt she could please her mother. For years Laurie also suffered from severe migraines, sometimes lasting two weeks at a time. With two young boys this made life difficult. She decided to take a risk and meet with some well-trained folks in our healing ministry to seek healing from her emotional wou nds.

As she relates,

In one particularly powerful healing session, Jesus appeared in the midst of a memory of my mother's verbal abuse and told me how much He loved me as His daughter. Another time, in a special church-wide healing service I sensed that my migraines might be the symptom of a performance-oriented mentality. Despite Jesus' previous affirming words to me, I still struggled with accepting the unconditional love He offered me and often evaluated myself on the basis of how well I felt I was performing as a mom and friend to others. During the service we had the opportunity to be prayed over by trained folks. I asked the woman praying over me to pray for my migraines. She had no knowledge of my emotional issues with my mother. At one point in her prayers, she stopped and looked at me and said, "You are a good mother. That's from the Lord not me." I was stunned to receive such a direct message from the Lord, not having raised any of the issues regarding my mom with this person, and yet God spoke through her directly to my performance orientation. The healing I have received has yielded abundant life—a foundational understanding of God's grace to me that has freed me from perfectionism in daily life. Setting aside the old fears and stress has also led to a dramatic drop in the incidence of migraines.

THE ROLE OF COURAGE IN RISK TAKING:

The well-known eighteenth century German poet Johann Wolfgang von Goethe is reported to have said, "There are many dangerous places in the world and one of them is safety." Dutch missionary Brother Andrew once commented, "We believers often say 'take care' when we should be saying: 'take risks.'"

Sadly, in today's western culture, courage seems to be a fading character trait. We don't want to offend. We don't like taking risks. We want to be safe. We don't want to be thought of as a fool. We have to ask, where is courage? Around our world men and women are dying for their beliefs. They are taking risks—both good and evil—daily. Yet too often we choose silence and safety. We have to ask ourselves, *What impact will our reticence have on our children and grandchildren?* Will they have the courage to stand for what is good and noble? Will they be willing to be fools for Christ or even go to jail or die for their faith? What can we do to nurture courage in the next generation?

Taking a risk involves courage and becoming a courageous person necessitates that we face our fears. I fear losing control. I fear moving out of a safe place. I fear the unknown consequences of the risk. The reality is I am not in control anyway nor can I guarantee safety. And I can't know the outcome of my risk taking.[4]

Our fear can paralyze us while courage will energize us. Courage comes from God. And God is plenty big enough to handle our fears. It helps to recognize that our fear, whatever the fear of the moment is, is impotent. God's power is not.

I have to remember it is God alone who is in control; He alone knows my future and He will not send me where He will not go with me. He will never ever abandon me or you. Period. (see Hebrews 13:5b)

WHAT IS YOUR RISK?

Jane, my friend in the opening story, faced two risks. Could she ever trust her husband again? And even more important, could she still trust God? In the midst of her pain she felt betrayed by God.

She was completely and utterly broken but in her brokenness she found grace. As she relates,

> The trees glistened from the nighttime ice storm as I walked alone in the mountains. My heart was broken and I was exhausted from holding the shattered pieces of our family together. I realized that not only did I feel betrayed by my husband, but I also felt deeply betrayed by God. I wept as I cried out to Him in this place of horrific pain. All I knew to do was to surrender, and as I did I found a God who was present even in this darkest place. The process of getting there did not require that I deny my pain or horror and outrage at the situation. In fact it was in embracing all of that, in the place of deep pain and sadness, that deep met deep and I was able to surrender all of it and find a God who was offering me a communion with Him for which I had always longed. Was it a risk

to trust? It was a huge risk with no guarantees, but stripped of everything but Him, I surrendered.

We can't see what will happen next in our lives, but God can see. He has perfect vision. He sees us in our frailty, our vulnerability. He sees our tears and cries with us. Our tears are precious to Him. Jesus' close friend Lazarus had become ill and died. His sisters asked Jesus to come quickly but by the time He arrived Lazarus had been in the tomb for four days. When Jesus came face to face with the tears of the sisters and their friends, He too began to weep. He already knew He was going to raise Lazarus from the dead but still, moved by the weeping of others, He also wept. He identified with their pain. Tears will come in this lifetime. Fears will plague us. But God can handle both. He understands.

Christ calls us to follow Him, and often He doesn't tell us where we are going. When I insist on knowing all the details, what the future holds, how things will work out, then what I'm really saying is, "God I'm not sure you've thought of everything." The reality is I think He needs my help. The reality is I've forgotten who He is and I don't believe He's big enough.

He is so much bigger than we can imagine. His love is so much greater. And He is calling each one of us to take a risk.

Your risk may be to trust Him for the very first time.

This was true for Nicodemus, a ruler of the Jews, who came to see Jesus at night. He sensed that God was with Jesus in an unusual way but he did not completely understand this. Jesus' response to him was, "Truly, truly,

I say to you, unless one is born again he cannot see the kingdom of God" (John 3:3).

If we want to see how big God is we too must be born again. We need the Holy Spirit to open our eyes.

Seeing God with new lenses begins when we receive Him as our personal Savior. We decide to lay aside fears and unanswered questions. To put our faith in Him and to begin the life-long journey of getting to know Him who loves us with a perfect love.

You may want to pray a prayer like this:

"Jesus I need you. I open the door to my heart and ask you to come in. Thank you for forgiving my sins. Thank you that you have promised never to leave me. Thank you, that at this moment, I can have the assurance that one day I'll be in heaven with you because of your sacrifice for my sins."[5]

If you prayed this prayer I encourage you to read Appendix 1 which contains a list of assurances that will encourage you and others with whom you share these truths.

You may be in a difficult season and your risk, like Jane's, is to choose to trust Him again, to cling to Him in a dark time.

It is a risk to say yes to Jesus but an even greater risk to say no.

When we say yes our eyes will be opened and we will see more clearly how very big our God is.

"Let us then with confidence draw near to the throne of grace that we may receive mercy and find grace to help in time of need" (Hebrews 4:16).

A TIME TO REFLECT:

1. Are you facing a risk in your own life at this time? What steps are you taking or will you take as you consider this risk?
2. Recall a time in the past when you took a risk. What were the results? What did you learn about God, about yourself?
3. Make a list of the ways you have experienced God's faithfulness in the past. Include the times you were not even aware of His presence. Looking back, how do you see His hand in that experience?

FOR FURTHER STUDY:

1. Read the "biography" of Moses. Look up Moses in the concordance of your Bible. Don't be daunted by the number of references. Take notes as if you were going to tell a young friend or a child the story of Moses. You might spend a week or a month doing this.
2. Re-read Exodus 3 and 4. What risk was God asking Moses to take? How do you think he felt? How did Moses respond? (See if you can discover how old he was at this time.) What were his fears? List the ways in which you identify with Moses.

List the ways in which God responded to Moses' fears. What have you learned about the character of God from this study? How might this apply to your life at this time, in the future?

SECTION 1 OVERVIEW

When I was in second grade my parents took me to an eye specialist. Apparently my teacher had mentioned to them that I seemed to be having trouble reading the blackboard. Mom and Dad had also noticed I was squinting a lot and wasn't able to read signs along the road. The ophthalmologist confirmed I was quite nearsighted. In fact I could barely read the big "E" on the chart. We left her office with a prescription for a very thick pair of ugly eyeglasses.

When my glasses arrived I was in for a shock. All of a sudden trees took on clarity I did not know existed. For the first time I could read the signs along the highway. Astonishingly, my teacher's notes on the blackboard made sense. From a distance I could recognize a friend in the hallway. Colors were vivid, lines were neat and clear, nature revealed a beauty I did not know existed. Instantly and dramatically my entire world changed.

I did not know what I had been missing.

Letters were clear but I just couldn't see them. God's scenery was actually crisp and vivid. It had only looked blurry to me. The problem was not with the object. It was with my eyes. My eyes distorted whatever I was looking at. I needed new lenses that would clarify what I was looking at and show it in its true reality.

I imagine you too have suffered from poor vision or have a family member who has eye problems. Many of us are nearsighted, farsighted, have an astigmatism, or a lazy eye. Some of us have experienced serious eye disease, have reached that glorious age when we need reading glasses, or even have trouble seeing at night. Perfect vision seems to be an anomaly in today's world.

Our vision of God can be a bit distorted too. We may realize it or we may not. When I first got glasses I simply could not believe what I could see. I never knew there was so much more.

In a similar way God is so much more than we recognize. Our view of Him can be distorted, way too small or blurry and superficial. Oh how He longs for us to see Him as He truly is.

It's helpful to ask ourselves: Do I long to see God's power increase in my life? Do I desire to really believe and walk in His pure love for me? Does my view of God need an infusion? No matter where we are in our faith journeys, I suspect each of us longs for a clearer picture of our big God. It's a risk worth taking.

How do we clarify our vision of God? Can we put on new lenses and see Him as He really is—all powerful, pure love, and completely sovereign?

Two factors are important to consider as we clarify our vision of God: We need a proper understanding of sin and a working knowledge of our enemy.

Chapter Three

MISUNDERSTANDING SIN CAN MESS US UP

R ecently I went to a mall near our home in metropolitan Washington DC. Six of my fun, young friends (each possessing a spirit of adventure) went with me. We had only one purpose—to ask random individuals who were in the mall two questions: What is your immediate response to the word "sin"? and How does the word "sin" make you feel?

Here are their unedited comments:

"Sin—oh gosh—guilt. It makes me feel judged." (21 year old female)

"Don't have one. If you are a sinner you're a sinner. It don't matter to me." (50 something male)

"Negative, I don't know." (20 something male)

"Oh God, my grandmother! (with laughter) It makes me feel unsettled more than anything." (21 year old female)

"Unfaithful, devastated. " (40 something female)

"This makes me feel it might be fun. It makes

me feel like I want to know more about what it is—curious like. I have to decide for myself not to do it." (20 something female)

"Sin equals my father. I feel anger." (male 25)

"Sin is misconception. People use it as a scapegoat. Everybody's view of wrong is different." (female 25)

"Hell, it feels bad." (50 something male)

"Everything—different people have ideas. It makes me feel uneasy, uncertain."(27 year old female)

"To do bad stuff." (11-year-old boy. His mother said she did not know.)

"It goes against God's will. It makes me feel overwhelmed." (20 something male)

"Being unholy depends on the situation." (30 something female.)

"All have sinned and fall short of the glory of God. The wages of sin is death, but the gift of God is eternal life through Jesus Christ." (A couple in their 70s)

"I want it. It feels good—for 5 minutes." (20 something male)

"That's the problem with the world today. Everyone tries to pull down the definitions of right and wrong and no one wants to stand up and take responsibility for actions or call sin sin." (48 year old female)

"Anything that separates us from God. It makes us feel bad because we are out of union with God." (40 year old female)

"Purgatory. It makes me feel dirty." (30 something male)

"Broken; it feels familiar." (36-year-old female)

Several results surprised me about our unscientific survey. First, almost every person was friendly and not the least bit offended by being asked their opinion about sin. In fact, most folks seemed delighted to be asked. This, in politically-correct, metropolitan Washington DC, surprised me. Had our purpose been different, I imagine we could have had some lengthy, fascinating conversations. It was obvious that "sin" is not a nice word. The word itself evokes condemnation, makes us uneasy about ourselves, and conjures up a sense of judgment.

None of this is popular in a society that idolizes tolerance.

Sin is frequently misunderstood. What does sin actually mean?

At its core sin is simply self-centeredness—a *me first* mentality.

In the biblical account of creation, Adam and Eve lived in the Garden of Eden, a paradise beyond our wildest dreams. However they became unhappy with their situation. Adam and his ravishing bride wanted more— even though they had been told it was deadly for them. They refused to listen to and obey a wise Father God who knew them and loved them and had prepared this perfect paradise for them. *They thought they knew better.* And so they disobeyed His instructions, went their own way, and through them sin entered the human race.

Any two or three year old reveals to us a humorous glimpse of self-centeredness. Perhaps you've seen the two-year-old creed:

"If it's mine, it's mine. If it's yours it's mine. If I like it is mine. If I can take it from you it is mine. If I am playing with something, all of the pieces are mine. If I think it is mine it is. If I saw it first it's mine. If I had it then put it down it is still mine. If you had it then you put it down it is now mine. If it looks like the one I have at home it is mine. If it is broken it is yours. "

My husband John is a minister. When he does premarital counseling he says to the couple, "You are about to find out how selfish you are." Several years ago he presided over the wedding of a beautiful, godly woman and a wonderful godly man. Six months later he asked the bride how things were going.

"John," she exclaimed, "When you told me I was about to find out how selfish I was, I was rather offended. But now I understand. Thinking about someone else's needs first on a daily basis is harder than I thought it would be! Now I realize I *am* instinctively selfish!"

The Bible defines this selfishness as sin, or separation from God. Not one of us is exempt. The Scriptures say, "Everyone did what was right in his own eyes" (Judges 17:6, 21:25). "For all have sinned and fall short of the glory of God" (Romans 3:23). Not one of us is innocent. Sin is man's declaration of independence from God. I particularly liked one girl's response to our survey question: "Sin equals broken. It feels familiar."

Our sinfulness has dire results. "For the wages of sin is death" (Romans 6:23). Sin results in separation from God. But there is good news. "But God shows His love for us in that while we were still sinners, Christ died for us" (Romans 5:8). We can be reconciled to God.

I believe there is a universal longing in the hearts of all men and women.

There is something in each of us that knows we are not pure. At our core we long to be clean, to be fixed, to be forgiven—perhaps because we know we're not? Whether we are a believer or an agnostic we know we don't have it all together nor do we always behave as we ought.

Often as we struggle with this concept of sin, we fall into one of three traps:

1. We Excuse Ourselves

Self-preservation seems to be instinctive. It is so easy to justify ourselves. It's second nature to rationalize our behavior.

It's also easy to blame others or our circumstances for our behavior.

We blame others—our spouses, our parents, our circumstances, our bosses, even our children. It might go like this: *If I had not come from such a messed up family I wouldn't ... if I had not suffered I wouldn't ... if my husband or wife would, then I could ... if only our circumstances were different ...* And our list goes on. Blaming others or our situations is a temporary fix. But this doesn't last and often leads to a critical spirit or to bitterness. It can become an excuse to avoid looking at our own errors. Yes, some have been horribly treated through no fault of their own. This is a different issue. But the majority of the time our natural tendency is to blame someone or something in the ordinary challenges of life in order to excuse our own attitudes or actions.

We compare ourselves to others. In this process we can create a false measuring stick to make us look better.

We say to ourselves, *Compared to others, I'm not so bad. At least I don't ... At least I'm not ... At least I haven't ... I know I would never ...*

Oh, but I would.

That murderer could be me. I remember when I realized this about myself. I was driving on a two-lane highway in the countryside of Virginia. The speed limit was fifty-five and I was pushing the limit. Alone with five small children in the car, I was in a hurry to get home. The grassy bank on my side of the road dropped off six or seven feet. There was not a lot of room to maneuver. Trying to focus in the midst of crying children, I noticed a car about a hundred yards ahead of me racing toward me in *my* lane. Furiously I began to honk and slow down. Distance between us evaporated. Panic set in. I did not know what to do. Do I get in the wrong lane to avoid him yet risk the chance of his moving over at the last minute, thereby colliding? Or do I turn and most likely roll over down the embankment avoiding a head on crash? There was no good option and no time to think. Terrified, I continued on, slowing as quickly as possible. At the very last minute, the guys in the car approaching me swerved into their proper lane, laughing, gesturing, and waving as they flew by me. At that moment, if I had had a loaded gun in my car I would not have hesitated to put it through my window and shoot those guys. They almost killed us. They could have killed my babies. And my mother hen instincts of protection were in rage. Murderer I could have become. No doubts.

I saw deep within my soul that I was capable of true evil, even if it seemed justified.

That lying CEO could be me. Doing income taxes can challenge our integrity. It's so easy to fail to report that little extra income, that honorarium that isn't reported on anyone else's forms. After all, we reason, it's not that big a deal anyway. It's just a little thing. Yet it is in the small areas of life that big decisions take root. Little compromises start the process of slowly unraveling our integrity, which grows over time. This slippage can lead to a loss of integrity, which results in frauds of all kinds. A few years ago, my husband John and I wrote a book, *Raising Kids With Character That Lasts,* which discusses eight character traits beginning with integrity.

I know how easy it could be for me to comprise in small ways—to sow the seeds of becoming that corrupt person.

That terrorist could be me. It was March of 2009 when "Jihad Jane" got the order on her computer screen to travel to Europe to kill Lars Vilks, a Swedish artist who had blasphemed the prophet Mohammad by sketching his face on the head of a dog. She was ready.

Jane's life had been one of pure misery. Repeatedly raped by her father, she ran away from home at the age of thirteen and lived on the streets. Cocaine, heroin, crack, and crystal meth were her companions. Married for the first time at sixteen, she suffered abuse, began gambling, and became an alcoholic and a prostitute. A one-night stand with a Muslim man began her interest in Islam, which she continued to pursue on the Internet, visiting Muslim websites and chat rooms. Here she found community. Soon she converted to Islam. Of her conversion, she remarked, "I was finally where I belonged." She felt the Muslims were just like her—underdogs. In time she was contacted by "EagleEye," an avowed jihadist, who gave her the opportunity to become a martyr. Now she was valued. And so in the spring of 2009 she boarded a plane to Europe to carry out her assignment and become a true terrorist. Fortunately she failed in her plans.[1]

What Jihad Jane intended was indeed horrific. But as I look at her background, the abuse, the pain, the lack of purpose, I ask myself, *How would I have responded if I had been raised the way she was? Could my anger and rage give birth to a twisted form of revenge?* I believe that I too would have longed for something to make sense out of my life, a group of people who made me feel special, something bigger than myself to get lost in, some way to make a difference, to right wrongs, a cause that would value my passion and call me to the nobility of one hundred percent commitment—even to death.

Yes, apart from the grace of God I too could have become a terrorist.

True humility is realizing what you are capable of.

God allows us to see what we are capable of in order to recognize how sinful we are. Often we don't even realize our capacity for evil. It has been hidden.

Recently I was in a hotel that had one of those fancy

make-up mirrors. In an effort to help us see ourselves better, the mirror is magnified ten times. And it reveals everything. I mean every blackhead, pimple, old age brown spot, filthy pore, deep wrinkle, and area discolored skin. Gross. I do not like these mirrors. I'd rather live with the illusion that I don't look so bad! But the reality is that the true me isn't as smooth and clean as I thought. The mirror reveals to me unpleasant details I have been denying, little blemishes I thought were hidden.

Oh how easy it is to make excuses for ourselves! Our personal pride is a strong force and an enticingly subtle trap.

2. WE CONDEMN OURSELVES

A second trap we fall into is that of condemning ourselves. We say to ourselves, *what I've done is just too bad. I can't even mention it. He can't forgive that, the lies, the men, the ...*

Oh, but He can. In fact He is waiting to. It is easy to confuse condemnation and conviction. Sin entered the world through Adam and Eve. The penalty for sin is death. This is what we deserve. But Jesus died on the cross in our place to pay this penalty. When I receive the gift of His death in my place I am freed from condemnation forever. Because He rose from the dead, conquering death, I too have the assurance of life after death with Him. When I accept Christ's sacrifice in my place I am born again. I am forgiven—completely. I have a clean slate. I have the promise that He will never leave me. I am no longer condemned—ever again.

In the reality of life, we too often fall back into self-condemnation. *I lost my temper again, I let that person down, I blew it again ...* We wallow around in the mud of self-condemnation, stuck and unable to move. We need a clear understanding of conviction. When we accept Christ's forgiveness of our sins and give our lives to Him, He gives us the powerful Holy Spirit to enable us to live this life on earth. One of the jobs of the Holy Spirit is to convict us of sin (John 16:8). The Scriptures also say that when we confess our sins, Jesus will forgive them, every one of them, and cast them as far as the east is from the west and remember them no more. (1 John 1:9, Psalm 103:12, Jeremiah 31:34). So our job is to listen to the Holy Spirit's conviction, confess the sin He points out, receive forgiveness, and determine to walk in a new way. This is repentance. There is no point wallowing in the mud of self- condemnation. Instead when we lose our temper, let someone down, blow it again in the same area, etc, our response should be to see this as the Holy Spirit convicting us of sin. We must confess it, receive Christ's forgiveness, and move on.

Once we are believers we have the wonderful promise, "There is therefore now no condemnation for those who are in Christ Jesus" (Romans 8:1).

Condemnation—no. Conviction—yes. Condemnation leads to death. But Jesus died in our place. Conviction can lead to repentance and forgiveness. We will explore this further in the next chapter.

It is hard to get our heads around this concept. It will take time but this is the heart of the gospel and it is **good** news.

When we say, *my sin is just too bad. He can't forgive me.* What we are really saying to God is, "Your Son's death isn't good enough for my sin. My sin is greater."

This is actually PRIDE clothed in self-pity. Am I telling God that the sacrifice of His only Son on the cross isn't good enough for me? That I need an encore? That I need something better?

Can you imagine how that makes our Father God feel?

Realizing this might cause you to want to pray:

"Oh God, forgive me for living as if my sins are more powerful than Your forgiveness. I accept your complete forgiveness for my sins of _____. I ask you to fill me with Your Holy Spirit and empower me to live the life You have called me to live."

3. WE TRY HARDER

This third trap sounds counterintuitive. There is an explanation. "We try harder" was once a great marketing slogan for a car rental agency. In the early sixties, after spending thirteen years in the red, the Avis Car Company hired a new president. To turn the company around, an advertising agency spent three months talking to the employees about the company. They asked a simple question: "Why does anybody ever rent a car from you?" The workers' reply made advertising history. "We try harder because we have to" became the new advertising slogan. Quickly this campaign changed the fortunes of Avis, taking the company from an amazing 11% of the market share to 35% in just four years.

Trying harder can be exactly what is needed in many situations, however this way of thinking can get us into trouble in the context of spiritual growth.

When I first became a Christian in college I was determine to live my new life well. Being a type A, driven person, I set out to succeed in living this Christian life. I worked hard at it and the harder I worked the more miserable I became. Finally I wrote to the guy who had led me to faith in Christ saying,

"I just wanted to tell you that I've really tried to be a good Christian. But it is so hard. I don't think I can do this. It may be great for you but it isn't working for me." I didn't think I would hear from him but I did and what he said truly surprised me:

> Susan, I understand completely. I remember feeling the same way. But living the Christian life is not about trying harder. It is about saying, "I can't Lord. I need you to do this in me." God gave us His Holy Spirit to enable us to live the life He has called us to live. We cannot do it by trying harder. Instead we have to go to Him saying, "I need You to do this in me." Growing as a believer is learning to rely on the power of the Holy Spirit within us rather than on ourselves to change us, to guide us, and to mold us."

It is easy to create false assumptions about the Christian life. *Now that I know Jesus I won't struggle so much, won't be tempted, won't sin; life will be a piece of cake* ... We create a "happily ever after life with Jesus" fantasy. But it's false. We will still be tempted. Jesus himself was tempted for forty days in the wilderness. We will still sin. We will suffer. But now we have understanding; we have forgiveness; and we have the power of the Holy Spirit at work within us.

It's also easy to let our failures discourage us. *I should know better. I shouldn't have done ... or I should have ... I'm too embarrassed to go to Him one more time about ...* And then we assume He can't or doesn't want to forgive us yet again. Once again we find ourselves acting as if our sins are too difficult for Him to handle. Once again we have become victims of our pride which says, "I should be able to conquer 'this.' whatever my 'this' of the moment is."

Sometimes it is our own human frailty that discourages us. Human frailty is not sin. God knows how frail we are for he made us. My friend Christie, a young mother of three, captures this tension between human frailty and sin:

> I need to be careful not to view my humanness (my physical limitations for example) as sin. It is not sinful for me to be tired at the end of a long day with my children, but how I respond to that human frailty can be sinful. When I have been up all night with a new baby and feel like such a failure during the day with my other two small children, my frailty might make me more vulnerable to sin, but my frailty is not itself a sin even though it makes me feel like a failure. Not being super mom, not having it all together, not achieving my view of what a perfect mom would be is not sin. It can lead to disappointment but it isn't necessarily sin. My frailty in the moment is my tiredness and my

inability to respond as a loving parent. It crosses the line to sin when I lash out in anger toward my child, or become bitter toward my situation.

Distinguishing between human frailty and sin is helpful. Sometimes we need to acknowledge our frailty as an inherent weakness and accept it even though we don't like it. And we need to be on the alert not to let our frailty develop into sin. Our frailty has a natural capacity to make us feel like failures.

In our failure, we might want to run from God. After all we are ashamed. The solution is not to run from Him but to race back to Him.

The Old Testament hero David experienced all of these feelings and temptations. He also committed adultery and murder. He lied and hid from God. He got very angry with God and he let Him have it! Yet, in spite of his sinning, God called him a "man after his own heart." How could this be? He was certainly not good. I believe it was because of his intimacy with God. Although David sinned greatly, when he came to his senses, he repented freely. His heart was genuinely broken over his behavior. He was completely honest with God. He held nothing back. Instead he told Him everything. His brokenness enabled him to experience a deep intimacy with the Father. When you are in a hard place, read the book of Psalms. You will be greatly encouraged by David's honesty.

We have a lot in common with David and with one another. We are all broken and in need of a savior. The Scriptures say "None is righteous, no, not one" (Romans 3:10).

But there is good news: "For while we were still weak, at the right time Christ died for the ungodly. For one will scarcely die for a righteous person—though perhaps for a good person, one would dare even to die—but God showed his love for us in that while we were still sinners, Christ died for us" (Romans 5: 6-8).

Jesus can handle your sin. He did it on the cross.

Do you remember a time when you disciplined your young child? On this particular occasion the child knew he had blown it. He had let you down, again. He had disobeyed you. He had even deceived you. For once he was broken-hearted. Sobbing in your arms he told you how sorry he was. Seeing your tears he cried even harder. In that moment what were your feelings toward your child? Disappointment, regret, relief? Perhaps. But even more I bet you were overwhelmed with tenderness and you simply wanted to hug him and comfort his little broken heart.

If we in our *imperfect* parental love would feel this way when our repentant, broken-hearted child comes to us, how much more does our heavenly Father enfold us in His arms, showering us with His abundant *perfect love* when we come to Him broken hearted over our own sin? Yes, he accepts us.

"My sacrifice, O God is a broken spirit; a broken and contrite heart O God you will not despise" (Psalm 51:17).

Our heavenly Father longs for us to confess our sins, to receive His forgiveness, and to sense His arms encircling us, crying with us, and receiving our broken hearts as a precious sacrifice. A broken heart can lead to a deep, precious intimacy with our heavenly Father who loves us more than we can ever imagine. His arms are outstretched, waiting to enfold you. Will you run into them?

"For I am sure that neither death nor life, neither angels nor rulers, nor things present nor things to come, nor powers, nor height nor depth, nor anything else in all creation, will be able to separate us from the love of God in Christ Jesus our Lord" (Romans 8:38-39).

A TIME TO REFLECT

1. How would you define sin?
2. Which trap did you most relate to? Why?
3. Explain the difference between conviction and condemnation. In what way might this be helpful to you or someone you know?
4. Is there anything in your life at this moment that is keeping you from running into the arms of God? Is there a truth in this reading that speaks to your issue?

FOR FURTHER STUDY:

1. Read Psalm 103, a Psalm written by David who was a great sinner and yet the one whom God called a "man after his own heart."
2. Go back and make a list of everything described in this passage that God has done for you.
3. Which verses demonstrate that God does know and understand us in a very personal way?
4. Look up Isaiah 43:1 & 25, Luke 5:31, 1 John 1:9, and other cross-references. How does this make you feel about man's sinful nature and God's desire to forgive?

Chapter Four

THERE'S AN ENEMY AND HE'S REAL

It started out as a normal conversation—a regular catching up between John and me at the end of the day. The kids were finally settled down in their rooms. Neither one of us had anything particular on our minds. We weren't aware of any big unresolved issue. And yet within ten minutes we were into a full-blown argument. We said things we shouldn't have. Feelings were hurt, assumptions took on a false reality, and marital conflict reared its ugly head.

What had happened? Obviously one of us said something that set off hurtful and defensive emotions. Feelings escalated into a painful encounter.

Where had this come from? Just ten minutes before, we had been fine. The abrupt change was just plain weird.

Later after we calmed down and took some time to reflect on what had happened, we asked, *what was that about?* It seemed as if a dark presence had slipped in unnoticed and surrounded us with a haze of resentment and defensiveness in a way that was out of all logical explanation.

It was as if an unseen enemy was trying to mess with

our marriage, to use whatever he could to bring us into a state of conflict.

In fact, this is precisely what had happened. And it wasn't to be the only time. Over the years in many different ways, we have experienced the truth of what the Scriptures teach—we do have an enemy. He is commonly referred to as the devil.

When someone hears the devil mentioned, their response can be one of two extremes.

Either we think too much of him or we think too little of him.

C. S. Lewis uses this phrase in his *Screwtape Letters* and it's still true today.

We all know people we might identify as a little crazy. They tend to see the devil around every corner. They blame everything on him and often disavow personal responsibility. An extreme focus on him can lead to imagined fears and dangers. On the other hand, it's not healthy to think too little of him. He does exist and it is a very naïve person who fails to acknowledge his role in the evil of this world and his attempts to influence us in our own lives.

I grew up in Chapel Hill, North Carolina, a small college town. My dad started taking me to Carolina football games when I was four years old. And I'll never forget the night UNC won their first national basketball title. I was in second grade and the final game against Kansas went to three overtimes! Our town went wild. Being a tomboy, I not only watched and cheered for my team, but I also played every sport I could. I remember sitting next to Dad in UNC's beautiful Kenan football stadium while he patiently explained the plays and pointed out the strengths and weaknesses of the opposing team—our enemy! Knowing the enemy's tactics was crucial to the game plan.

In a similar way we must study our enemy in order to develop a realistic plan to defeat him. Three questions will help us: Who is he? How does he work? How should we respond to him?

WHO IS HE?

A good coach will study the personality, the strategy, and the tactics of the next opposing team. He will not rely completely on hearsay but will send his assistant coaches or scouts to get a firsthand look at the opposition. In a similar way, we can go directly to the source, the Bible, to gain firsthand knowledge of our enemy. In God's Word we will discover several truths about the enemy.

He is real. He is first described as an angel who rebelled against God (Isaiah 14:12, Luke 10:1). Throughout both the Old and New Testaments we see individuals who encounter his wrath. There are approximately fifty-three references to him in Scripture. He is called by many names—serpent, Satan, devil, enemy, etc. Jesus Himself was led into the wilderness by the Holy Spirit, where He was tempted by the devil for forty days and nights. The devil is evil personified.

He is the enemy. The apostle Peter says, "Your enemy the devil prowls around like a roaring lion seeking someone to devour" (1 Peter 5:8).

He is aggressive not passive. A roaring lion is not passive. He is on the prowl.

He's a liar. Jesus Himself describes the devil as, "a liar and the father of lies" (John 8:44).

He disguises himself as an angel of light (2 Corinthians 11:14). Satan twists the truth so that it sometimes presents itself as good. Oh, how we see this in our culture today.

He's defeated. John says, "For he who is in you [referring to Christ] is greater than he who is in the world [referring to Satan]" (1 John 4:4). This is great news indeed!

If we recognize the personality traits of the enemy we will be more equipped to know how to defeat him and less likely to be fooled by him.

HOW DOES HE WORK?

In prepping for a football game a wise coach will pay attention to the type of formation the opposing team is most likely to use and he will look for any adjustments they might make. He wants his own team to be prepared for any eventuality and ready to launch a counter attack.

In a similar way, it helps to identify several ways in which our opposition will seek to engage us.

1. He is the tempter.

Temptation in itself is not wrong. Jesus was led by the Spirit into the wilderness where He spent forty days being tempted by the devil (Matthew 4, Luke 4). If Jesus Himself was tempted we should not be surprised when this same enemy tempts us. In fact, the writer to the Hebrews tells us that Jesus was tempted in every way that we will be yet He did not sin (Hebrews 2 and 4).

2. He twists the truth.

One of Satan's favorite tricks is to quote Scripture but to misuse it. He did this to Jesus.

"If you are the Son of God, command this stone to become bread" (Luke 4:4). Of course Jesus was the Son of God and He was hungry. But that did not make it right for Him to turn stones into bread. It might have sounded good but this was not the way God intended to reveal that Jesus was indeed His Son. It was a short cut.

It's easy to quote a Bible verse to give us permission to do something we know is wrong. We have to be very careful that we are not taking Scripture out of context or twisting it to satisfy our own desires.

Ask yourself, *would my action be contrary to God's will?* It helps to remember God does not lead us contrary to His word. A friend of mine whose career necessitates much travel said to me,

"Susan, I recently had the thought that maybe there is someone out there who is better for me than my wife. Do you think that could be God saying that?" "No," I replied. "God does not lead contrary to Scripture and He has called you to be faithful to your wife." The voice he heard was from the enemy, not the Savior.

It is comforting for us to note how Jesus was tempted. Much can be learned from a more complete study of this found in Luke 4.

3. He is the accuser.

In the previous chapter we talked about the difference between conviction and condemnation. When the Holy Spirit convicts us of our sin and we confess it and ask for forgiveness, we are forgiven. Satan, however, loves to condemn. And he often does it by way of bringing up old sins again and again.

You really blew it when you lost your temper with your child. You may have permanently damaged her. When you had that abortion you destroyed a life. You can't be forgiven for having sex with that person. You knew better.

If we have sincerely confessed our sin and received His forgiveness, Jesus has chosen not to remember our sin ever again (Psalm 103:12, Jeremiah 31:34, 1 John 1:9). Therefore, we must not listen to the accuser. In fact we should say to the enemy, "What are you talking about? I am forgiven. This has been forgotten. I am clean." You may not *feel* clean. Healing takes time. But the fact is you *are clean.* **What God declares is much truer than what you feel.**

4. He speaks in generalities.

You are no good. You'll never amount to anything. You won't make it in your career. You are a lousy wife. You have probably ruined your child. You'll never have friends ...

Sound familiar?

It has helped me to recognize that Satan often speaks generally whereas the Holy Spirit convicts specifically. Ask yourself, is this a specific conviction? If so it is likely the prompting of the Holy Spirit and you need to confess. *I shouldn't have said what I did and I need to ask God's forgiveness and for forgiveness from the person I offended.*

If, on the other hand, it is general mud being slung at you, it's likely the enemy. Ignore him or tell him to go to hell where he belongs!

5. He is subtle.

One of the reasons Satan is so dangerous is that he is subtle. And my heart is so easily deceived. I experience this in what I call the 3 D's, although there are many more than three! He *disguises*, he *discourages,* and he *distracts.*

He disguises. When John and I so easily fell into the argument I described at the beginning of the chapter, our gut reactions were to blame each other. There were plenty of faults we could list. I'm sure we could have conjured up hurts and grievances from over forty-six years without much effort! However the issue wasn't either of us; it was the unseen presence of our enemy who wanted to take advantage of two naturally sinful people who were absolutely exhausted. Simply recognizing what was happening was a big insight for both of us. It enabled us to recognize a danger from the outside and enabled us to quit accusing one another. Instead we joined forces to pray for the protection of our marriage. Make no mistake, our enemy is determined to destroy marriages. Now of course we can't blame the enemy for everything. That would be taking things too far. But too often we fail to recognize his disguise or his presence at all.

He discourages. Discouragement often comes in the form of the "if onlys." "If only" my child weren't so difficult, "if only" I did not come from an abusive home, "if only" my husband understood, "if only" I had a husband, "if only" I could get a better job, "if only" I had her life ... Each of us can come up with a list of "if onlys." The reality is that the "if onlys" is a sickness of self-pity. And its ultimate result is discouragement. In our malaise we underestimate God. The things making us miserable become greater in our minds than our God. And this mentality thrills our enemy.

He distracts. We know there's something we should be doing. But we just can't seem to get to it. That letter of apology, or thank you note, that task we've been putting off, our Bible study or prayer time, even time alone to connect with our spouse. *Life is so busy, I'll do that when things calm down,* we reason. But life will not calm down. It just gets more complicated. Often in his subtlety the enemy will distract us from what really matters in order to get us to settle for things that are secondary.

6. He mischaracterizes God.

Satan will attribute feelings and falsehood to God that are contrary to His character and His Word. A single friend lamented, "God understands how I feel. It's hard being single. He gave me sexual desires. I need to feel loved. It's ok to have sex. This person may be *the one.* Surely God wants me to be happy."

God does understand how we feel, how hard abstinence is. Yet He has created us for something better than the temporary happiness that sin brings. The disillusionment and pain that follow are great. God says sex is designed to be between a man and a woman in marriage—period. His laws are for our own good. God never leads contrary to His word. Remember, Satan can quote Scripture but he always misuses it.

7. He produces an unhealthy fear.

In all honesty I really struggle with this one. I have a vivid imagination. This can be good when used for His creative purposes or devastating when the enemy gets control of it and I fall prey to extreme worry. My child is late and I am sure there's been a car accident. Or I have a headache and I know it's a brain tumor. Often fear is expressed in a case of the "what ifs?" *"What if" I don't get that promotion? "What if" I never get married? "What if" my child is born with defects? "What if ... ?"* One of the enemy's tricks is to get us to trust God for tomorrow on today's faith. God has given us faith for today. Tomorrow we will be different people. He gives us grace for the moment. One day, one minute at a time. But it is always enough.

My friend Lyn suffered from cancer. When she completed her treatment she had to wait six months for her next checkup. On the day of her appointment she was understandably nervous. I prayed with her on the phone. After her appointment she called, "Susan," she exclaimed, "I'm clean. I'm clean!" We rejoiced together but then her voice became quiet, "But what if next time the report is bad?"

"Lyn," I replied, "Do not listen to that voice. That is the enemy Satan. He is a joy-robber. At this moment he is trying to steal your joy." We need to rejoice in today rather than be consumed by fear of tomorrow. Our God is the loving God of today and the sustaining God of tomorrow.

HOW SHOULD WE RESPOND TO HIM?

It is two weeks until the Super Bowl. This year the two teams who will meet already played in regular season. They are familiar with one another's weaknesses and strengths. Even so, players and coaches have studied films, prepared an array of defenses and are busy creating new offensive tactics. The right response is crucial. They want to draw on their own strengths, take advantage of the opponent's weaknesses and thereby ensure they go home with the great trophy! We too need the right approach in responding to our opposition. Three things will help—recognize him, resist him, and remember who you belong to.

1. Recognize him

The defensive guards on the football team have to watch the quarterback's eyes. A subtle shift of his eyes can indicate exactly where he might pass the ball. Then an alert defender can move in for the interception or tackle. Here are two keys to enable us to recognize how our enemy might work.

Be on the alert.

I was having coffee with four women, all deeply committed believers, when one of the women shared something startling:

> I need to tell you that I've become attracted to a man who is not my husband. He works in the same business as my husband so we are thrown together a lot socially. He's a poet and, as you all know,

I'm an artist. I find that we are gravitating to each other. He seems to understand me better than my husband does. We are talking on the phone during the week. Nothing has happened yet but I know I'm treading on dangerous ground. I need to ask you to hold me accountable to end this relationship.

A shocked silence settled like a thick cloud over the table. And then her phone rang. Turning her back to us she stood up to take the call as the rest of us began to talk. Out of the corner of my eye, I noticed her face turn to us, drained of color. Looking at us she took a deep breath and turning back to her phone she said,

"I need to ask you not to call me again, ever. Our relationship is not going in a healthy direction. We must end this. Thank you. "

In the ensuing silence we knew we were standing on holy ground. How good of God that He would allow the man to call her right when she had shared her temptation with us and as we sat there with her to hold her accountable. My wise friend was alert to the temptation in her face. She chose to share it with us because she knew she needed support to resist it. She chose to flee temptation. We must flee temptation, not flirt with it! (1 Corinthians 6:18, 1 Timothy 6:11, etc.)

Learn your vulnerable points.

I have found that I'm most vulnerable to the attacks of the enemy when I'm exhausted. Or if I am juggling too many balls, the stress makes me fragile. If I've been several days without time alone with God to pray and read His Word, I am vulnerable. Different seasons in life bring unique vulnerable points. Pregnancy caused me to turn into a crazy woman. As a young mom, being shut up with five little children in the middle of winter made me vulnerable. Today, as an older woman (not *old* mind you!), I find I can't multitask the way I once could. Multitasking on various levels used to give me an exhilarated rush. Today it exhausts me and makes me crabby. A change in seasons can be a time of vulnerability. That first baby, a new job, romantic breakup, a move, a family illness, a family crisis, menopause, an empty nest.

Our friends Jim and Sally experienced a family crisis. They are the parents of two boys raised in a strong loving Christian family. But when their son Mac was seventeen they got the call every parent dreads. The phone rang at midnight and the policeman said,

> "We have your son Mac. He is alright but we have him in jail. We picked him up driving and drinking and discovered drugs in the car as well. He is now in custody." Hanging up the phone, Jim and Sally knew their life was about to change— drastically. In a moment of supernatural wisdom, Jim looked at Sally and said, "We do not know what is ahead. We are in real trouble. But whatever is ahead we must not let our marriage become a casualty as well. We are going to stop right now and recommit ourselves to each other in marriage."

This step of recommitment was to be crucial in the weeks ahead as they discovered Mac had been abusing drugs and alcohol since he was fourteen. Jim and Sally reacted differently to the crisis. Jim went into Mr. Fix-it mode while Sally cried. They grieved differently. The family went through two hard years of counseling and rehab. Their marriage was tested. However, they relied on the renewal promises they had made in their time of vulnerability. It served them well. Ten years later we were with Mac and his family to celebrate a decade of sobriety and today he is a godly man with an amazing wife and the father of four. Let their story give you hope!

2. Resist him

One of the most encouraging promises in Scripture is found in James 4:7, "Submit yourselves therefore to God. Resist the devil and he will flee from you." Bible teacher Beth Moore once said that it helps to resist him out-loud. He does not have the power to read our thoughts although he does know our weakness. So if she feels under attack she says out loud, "Leave me Satan." Sometimes in my own life when I'm feeling under attack I say out loud, "Satan by the power of the Holy Spirit who lives within me, I command you to leave me. You have no right to me. I belong to Jesus. So leave immediately!"

My friend Craig says if he senses a dark presence coming between him and his wife that he turns his head and says out loud, "Get away from us." This helps him remember that Satan is the enemy, not his wife. And sometimes it causes them to burst out laughing instead of getting into an argument.

3. Remember: You belong to Christ.

If we asked Christ to come into our lives we belong to Him. (See appendix#1)

"Little children you are from God and have overcome them, for he who is in you is greater than he who is in the world" (1 John 4:4). What a powerful, powerful promise. Another one is found in a letter from the apostle Paul. "No temptation has overtaken you that is not common to man. God is faithful, and he will not let you be tempted beyond your ability, but with the temptation he will also provide the way of escape, that you may be able to endure it" (1 Corinthians 10:13). Jesus understands our temptation. He Himself has experienced every temptation that we ever will. We can choose His path of escape. The question is, will we? It helps to remember who we belong to.

Never forget: Compared to the power of Christ, Satan is completely impotent.

In this world we are going to have trouble. Jesus reminds us, "In the world you will have tribulation. But take heart; I have overcome the world" (John 16:33).

In this world we must identify our enemy, recognize how he works, and learn how to respond to him. It's a lifelong process and it's messy and exhausting. Just like the players in the football game, we will get bruised and bloody. However there is good news! We already know we have won! We don't have to wait to find out the final score. The victory is already determined. The opposition has been defeated. We have won. At this moment, we can raise our arms to the sky cheering with the world championship trophy.

This is the ultimate victory—the story of Jesus.

A TIME TO REFLECT:

1. What did you learn from this chapter that clarified or enhanced your knowledge of the enemy?
2. When are you most vulnerable to his attacks? How might he try to trip you up?
3. What will be helpful to you in the future in recognizing the enemy and standing against him?
4. Do you need to share with a trusted friend a specific way in which you are tempted and have her (or him if you are a man) pray for you, encourage you, and hold you accountable to stand firm?
5. List the promises and ways in which you can count on God to defend you. Read 1 John 4:4 and Jeremiah 50:34 to get started, but make your own list.

FOR FURTHER STUDY:

1. Read Luke 4. What happened to Jesus just prior to His being led into the wilderness? (See Luke 3:21-23.) Who led Jesus into the wilderness? What significance might this have?
2. List the ways Jesus was tempted by Satan. What subtlety did Satan use? How did Jesus respond to him? Why do you suppose Jesus had to have this awful experience? (Hint: see Hebrews 2:14-18 and Hebrews 4: 14-16.)
3. What do you learn from the temptations of Jesus that is an encouragement to you?

The name of the Lord is a strong tower; the righteous man runs into it and is safe. (Proverbs 18:10)

SECTION 2 OVERVIEW

Our eye doctor's expression was grave. The news he had for my husband was not good.

"John," he said, "You have a rare eye disease. It's called keratoconus. The cornea in your eye has grown into the shape of a cone rather than that of a ball. Your disease is advanced and in order to retain sight in your eye you will need a corneal transplant." After much consultation, we came to the realization that if John didn't receive a transplant he would likely go blind in the eye. And his other eye had begun to show early signs of the disease as well.

He was put on the transplant list at John's Hopkins Wilmer Eye Clinic. And the wait began—a sobering wait for we knew that in order for John to get a new cornea someone had to die. He was given a pager to wear at all times so that when the call came that a cornea was available he would be able to get to the hospital in time. The week before Easter, Holy Week, the beeper went off. On the Friday before Easter, John went into surgery to receive his new cornea. Our emotions were all mixed up—joy that the surgery was successful and he would now be able to see and yet a profound sadness that someone had had to die in order that he might see. This irony of this happening on Good Friday—the day of Jesus' crucifixion—was overwhelming for both of us.

When John got his new cornea he immediately saw things differently. The damaged old cornea had been removed. A new one was stitched in place. He still had healing that needed to occur. He was cautious in what he did, a bit unsure. But as time went by he became used to his new vision. He began to see things with a clearer focus. There was richness in what he saw that he had never imagined.

John's old cornea was an obstacle to clear vision. It had become a barrier—preventing him from seeing things in their true beauty. In a similar way, we have seen how confusion about sin and a misunderstanding of our enemy can become barriers to a clear view of our amazing God. Now it's time to move on to five ingredients that will enable us to gain a bigger view of God and to enjoy Him more and more each day. We too have been blind but now we can begin the journey of learning to see with new lenses.

Open our eyes, Lord.

CHAPTER FIVE

WHAT AM I GOING TO BASE MY LIFE ON? IT WILL BE SOMETHING

What or who is your ultimate authority? To whom do you go when you need advice? What sources or people have helped to form your philosophy of life? What are your priorities for living? What is your main passion?

Why does having an ultimate authority matter? What if I don't want one?

These are big questions, important questions. Questions that call for a thoughtful response.

The fact of life is that all of us live under authority already. The laws of physics in our natural world impose authority upon us. For example, we live under the authority of gravity. Total freedom would mean freedom from the constraints of gravity, but if we try to jump off a wall and fly we quickly realize that freedom doesn't exist. Complete freedom is not a choice any of us can make, no matter what our faith or lack of faith declares.

Bob Dylan a folk-rock singer who made it big in the sixties wrote a famous song titled "You Gotta Serve Somebody." His lyrics begin,

You may be an ambassador to England or France
You may like to gamble, you might like to dance,
You may be the heavyweight champion of the world
You may be a socialite with a long string of pearls.
But you're gonna have to serve somebody, yes indeed
You're gonna have to serve somebody,
It may be the devil or it may be the Lord
But you're gonna have to serve somebody.

Dylan's point is that whether we like it or not we are under authority and serving someone.

Many of you know the name Elizabeth Gilbert. She is the author of the bestselling memoir *Eat, Pray, Love*, which was made into a popular movie starring Julia Roberts.

The book chronicles a spiritual journey that begins with internal torment and ends with discovery of God. It is, in many ways, a classic conversion story. Except that there is a twist. The god whom Gilbert discovers is not the God of the Bible, or one of the many gods of Hinduism, nor even the god of Islam. The God she discovers is the god within herself.

Gilbert's spiritual awakening occurs when she realizes that, as she writes, "God dwells within you as you yourself, exactly the way you are." She goes on to explain that, "somewhere within us all, there does exist a supreme self who is eternally at peace. That supreme self is our true identity, universal and divine." Her personal goal, therefore, as a spiritual being, is to "honor the divinity that resides within me."

This way of speaking about God may sound shocking in the present context, but there is a reason Gilbert's book spent more than three years on the New York Times bestseller list. Faith in the supposed god within is intensely attractive because it requires nothing of us but to discern our deepest desires and then fulfill them.

All too often even Christians fall into a form of this god-within theology when we look to our desires or internal feelings to lead us rather than to the guidance of Scripture when seeking to order our behavior and priorities.

To this idea that "God lies within and is waiting to be found," the first chapter of Genesis cries out, "No!" He stands apart and before. He has no beginning. He speaks and galaxies come into being. He is not found in you or in me, or in the beauty of a sunset. You and I and the sunset all find our place *in Him*.

Creation is God's. And if creation is God's then we are God's. If we want to know ourselves and to understand ourselves we need to know our maker.[1]

Assuming the role of God in our own life and thus placing ourselves as the ultimate authority only leads to misery.

It is difficult in today's world to determine what or who will be our authority on how we should live. Indeed, many in our post-modern culture would say there is no authority. Instead they argue each must find his or her own authority and whatever a person finds can quickly change. It's a variable. Authority becomes the flavor of the month, the choice of the day, whatever or whomever fits your needs of the moment.

It's not unlike Paul's experience in Athens when he found an altar to "An Unknown God." The Greeks were trying to cover all their bases, even the unknown ones.

Paul was quick to capitalize on their uncertainty and proclaim to them the one true God. (See Acts 17:22-34)

DECIDING AUTHORITY

This good news is for us as well. There is one God, one authority: The almighty God, the King of kings. Jesus said of Himself, "I am the way, the truth and the life. No man comes to the Father except through me" (John 14:6).

And there's more great news. He's given us the Word of God, the Scriptures, where we can go to learn about Him and to see how He would have us live and to make sense of our world.

THE RELIABILITY OF SCRIPTURE AS THE SOURCE OF AUTHORITY

But wait a minute. Just the phrase "authority of Scripture" brings up all sorts of questions. Can we take the Bible literally? What about the contradictions that seem to be there? How can we know it is true? Even scholars disagree over many aspects of Scripture so how are we supposed to know who is right, what is correct? There is not universal agreement on all of the Bible's teachings.

The intention of this book is not to present arguments for the reliability of the Scriptures. Others have done this much better. Two thoughtful books are: *Evangelical Truth* by John Stott and *Taking God at His Word: Why the Bible Is Knowable, Necessary, and Enough and What That Means for You and Me* by Kevin De Young.

Instead, my purpose is to encourage you to give God your doubts and trust that He is big enough to handle them. And in a step of faith, take a risk to believe that God's Word is true and experience its power to change your life.

Ultimately deciding that God is our authority and His Word is the truth is a choice each one of us has to face. We cannot remain indecisive.

Indecision is like sitting on a fence and over time that fence becomes really uncomfortable. Our bottoms will become sore or numb and eventually we'll either jump off or fall off. The question is: Do I fall on the side of choosing to believe the authority of Scripture or slide off the other side of the fence into a life of shifting allegiances, none of which will ultimately satisfy and bring peace.

In his autobiography, Billy Graham shares the story of his own difficulty in accepting the authority of the Scriptures. One of Billy's best friends, Chuck, was attending seminary while Billy was getting ready for one of his first crusades. For many years they'd prayed together, shared in ministry together, and become the closest of friends, but now Chuck was raising questions which in turn caused Billy to question.

Could he believe the authority of Scripture? Was the Bible relevant in the face of problems too hard to resolve? Must an intellectually honest man know everything about the Bible's origins before he could use it? One evening in 1949, Billy went for a walk alone in the forest. He describes this night:

The moon was out. The shadows were long

in the San Bernardino Mountains surrounding the retreat center. Dropping to my knees there in the woods, I opened the Bible at random on a tree stump in front of me. I could not read it in the shadowy moonlight, so I had no idea what text lay before me. Back at Florida Bible Institute, that kind of woodsy setting had given me a natural pulpit for proclamation. Now it was an altar where I could only stutter into prayer. The exact wording of my prayer is beyond recall, but it must have echoed my thoughts; "Oh God! There are many things in this book I do not understand. There are many problems with it for which I have no solution. There are seeming contradictions. There are some areas in it that do not seem to correlate with the modern science. I can't answer some of the philosophical and psychological questions Chuck and others are raising." I was trying to be on the level with God but something remained unspoken. At last the Holy Spirit freed me to say it, "Father, I am going to accept this as Thy Word, by faith. I'm going to allow faith to go beyond my intellectual questions and doubts, and I will believe this to be your inspired Word." When I got up from my knees that night my eyes stung with tears. I sensed the presence and power of God as I had not sensed it in months. Not all my questions were answered, but a major bridge had been crossed. In my heart and mind I knew a spiritual battle in my soul had been fought and won.[2]

We too have to make a choice—to believe in the authority of God's word or to reject it. We can't have it both ways. We will fall off the fence.

Making a choice to accept the authority of the Scriptures does not mean I have to become an obnoxious person, quoting Bible verses to solve every problem. It does not mean I am committing intellectual suicide. Nor does it mean that now I will have all the answers.

Instead, what I do have is a firm foundation. I've jumped off the fence onto a very strong rock that is huge, firm, and unmovable. From this place I will hunger to learn more, to study. I won't be afraid to question and I learn to live by faith when there are no easy answers.

THE IMPORTANCE OF MYSTERY

Mystery is a crucial ingredient of faith. There will always be aspects of God, Jesus, the Holy Spirit, and the Scriptures that we do not comprehend. Life will not always make sense and how God works or does not work can be disappointing. If we could answer everything about God and explain Him it would lower Him to the level of man. He would no longer be God. Mystery is important. Unanswered questions are okay. In times like this we choose to trust. What we don't understand is not nearly as important as what we can know to be true. Mystery is an important facet of experiencing the bigness of God.

When I find I am stuck with a question or an unresolved issue I ask God to either give me an answer or give me a peace about living with the question. If no answer comes I simply put the question on my "heaven list" and determine that I'll ask Him to answer it when I get there. And then I move on. This is the exercise of spiritual faith. We exercise faith in many areas of life. I fly and I could not tell you how the plane stays up in the air, nor assure you that it will. I do not understand aerodynamics, yet I fly on planes. It is a different type of faith.

Once we chose to accept Scripture as the authority for our lives we will want to become a student of the Word.

WHY SPEND TIME IN GOD'S WORD?

Recently I asked several different friends why God's Word was important to them. Here are a few of their answers:

> Studying God's Word is important for me because it is foundational to knowing who God is and I want to know Him, to be in relationship with Him within the circle of my life and my calling. Secondly I want to think rightly about life, from His point of view, in all its many aspects. It's a compass orientation.

> It started out with a desire for a better understanding of life, myself, and God. It ended up with being a love affair with Him, wanting to be with Him more, get Him better, hunker down with Him in my inmost parts. And then it sometimes circles back around to what He can give to me,

more wisdom and guidance (which I need every day). And back to gratitude and love and hunkering down. The astounding thing is that He, even the God of the universe, reaches my own heart and warms me there. Go figure. We can't figure. (That's mystery.) We just get to receive.

There's a reason why my new smart phone came with an instruction manual, but do I have to read it? No, maybe not, but will I ever get any further than the power button? Can't I do it by myself? In my case that would be pretty risky. And it's not unlike everyday living, risky without direction. God designed me with infinite potential, but I'll never know what it is until I dig into His instruction manual. His word is the only way to fully live each day, to share in who He is, joyfully, graciously, tirelessly. God's got an 'app' for everything.

When I study God's word, I'm primarily reminded of my identity: I'm Christ's. That said, because of my work as an English teacher, I also find that I'm reminded of the power of story through studying the Word of God. When I read the stories given to us by God in the Bible, I remember why it is important for me to teach good stories to students. I'm reminded of how deeply God cares for humanity when I read through the arc of the Bible. Because God has shown such love to humans, to me, I can therefore strive to show love to my students.

Studying God's Word is important to me because it reminds me of who God is, of who I am, and of where we are headed—together. It imports meaning into the little moments I spend with children all day long. And it reminds me of a bigger story than the one I see right in front of me, a better story that I am called to live into. Studying the word keeps me excited because the deeper I move into it, the more I taste: 'But we impart a secret and hidden wisdom of God, which God decreed before the ages for our glory' (1 Corinthians 2:7). I connect with a deeper purpose for my life than the obvious ones that demand my attention during the day. Also, the more familiar I am with His words, the more likely they are to rise above my own. To make His thoughts, my thoughts, His words, mine; that is my longing! The quicker I can connect with His thoughts about a situation I am facing, the easier it is for me to deal with it. It's kind of like the first time I walked out of the optometrist's office with glasses on and the world offered depth and clarity that I had been missing when I walked in. I could see! When I encounter the Spirit of God over the pages of Scripture, I literally feel that fire in my bones that Jeremiah spoke of. I open the pages and find my life in them and it is motivating.

And I love this one:

"I just don't work well without it!"

HIS WORD IS THE ULTIMATE TRUTH

There are so many practical ramifications of His truth:

His Word does not change and it applies with equity to every person regardless of gender, social standing, race, culture, age, or knowledge.

How we *do* church (evangelize, worship, and serve) will vary from culture to culture and season to season. Methods must be fluid. But the message should never change. Who are we to think we should alter the Word of God? Not changing the message helps us to distinguish between message (His Word) and methods (the means of proclaiming it). His Word has supernatural power. "For the word of God is living and active. Sharper than any two-edged sword, piercing to the divisions of soul and of spirit, of joints and of marrow, and discerning the thoughts and intentions of the heart" (Hebrews 4:12).

We have to grasp the fact that God's Word has the same power that was used to raise Jesus from the dead. His Word is not just words, nor is it merely wise sayings. It is possessed, filled, and backed by the enormous power of the Holy Spirit.

His Word is our ultimate guidebook and power source for life.

Thankfully God did not call us to follow Him and then leave it up to us to figure out how to do it. He has not placed us in a world of conflicting values and expected us to guess. Instead He has given us His Word to be a "Lamp to my feet and a light to my path" (Psalm 119:105).

One of the main prayers I pray for my children and grandchildren is that they would fall in love with the

Word of God. I long for His Word to become their ultimate guide, their power source. I will leave them, their dad will leave them, mentors will leave; all of us will die. Yet His Word will remain until it is fulfilled upon His return. The greatest gift we can give our kids, grandkids, those we mentor, and our friends is a hunger and trust in the power and authority of His Word.

If we want our picture of God to become larger, we must spend time in His Word.

BEWARE OF SUBSTITUTES

There can be a tendency in the social or educational circles we run in to read great books, create detailed journal entries, discuss deep ideas and challenges, impress each other with wisdom, and debate great theological or social issues. This is good to a point. Yes, God can use it but we must take care that it doesn't become a subtle substitute for the Word of God.

I've heard Bible teacher Beth Moore say it like this, "If in our pursuit of greater theological knowledge God has gotten smaller, we've been deceived. Unintentionally, but deceived all the same."

Men give insights; God gives power, wisdom, and supernatural peace.

There was once a godly man who prayed for many years for his faith to grow. For a long time he did not see any growth in his faith. One day he opened his Bible and read, "So faith comes from hearing and hearing through the word of Christ" (Rom 10:17). He began to study his

Bible and his faith grew.

The apostle Peter encouraged his friends to be "like newborn infants, long for the pure spiritual milk, that by it you may grow up to salvation" (1 Peter 2:2).

If we desire to grow in our faith and to help others acquire a firm faith, knowing and utilizing God's Word in our own lives is essential. In a world of shifting cultural values there is one authority that stands the test of time—God's Word. As we grow in our own respect and deference for His Word, we will find ourselves naturally imparting this to those around us.

MY STORY

When I was young I tried reading the Bible. Of course I began in the beginning. Wasn't that where you started all books? I'd make it a little ways until I got to the fifth chapter of Genesis and the list of names began. My eyes would begin to droop and my attention wandered. What I was reading was boring. I didn't see how it had anything to do with me. So for years my old, black, King James family Bible gathered dust on my closet shelf.

It wasn't until I was a college student that I understood the richness of the Word of God and discovered it was full of practical application for my own life. Soon after I accepted Christ I became friends with Ricky. A college basketball player, Ricky seemed to have everything going for him. He was interesting to talk to and fun to be with. In getting to know him, I became aware of a depth to his personality that I could not explain. He had a deep assurance about his faith and an amazing ability to relate it to ordinary, everyday situations. He was excited about God's Word. To him, God's Word was alive and relevant. It was not outdated and it spoke to him. I was curious and frankly wondered if we were reading the same book. I shared my own frustrations with him and he taught me how he studied the Bible. We began in the Gospel of Luke. To make it easier, we drew three columns on a blank piece of paper. One column we titled "verse," one "observation," and one "application." First we wrote out the verse word for word under the verse column. Then after reading the verse several times we wrote things we noticed in the observation column. In doing this we asked ourselves questions about the verses: how, what, when, where, why? Finally, as we reflected on the observations, we considered the application. Was there anything here that applied to my life right now or that might in the future? We listed any personal applications that came to mind. At first I felt awkward with this method of Bible study. But as I persisted over a period of time, I grew in confidence and saw God speaking clearly to me through His Word. Slowly the Scriptures became relevant to my everyday life.

I began to set aside time first thing in the morning for a quiet time (a time in which to pray and study the Scriptures). Nearly fifty years later I continue this habit. It has revolutionized my life. Each morning I begin with reading a Psalm and a Proverb. I put a check by the Psalm so I'll know where to go to the next day. For Proverbs I simply match the chapter number of the Proverb to the date. I look for promises from God and descriptions of His character traits. It has been said that there are over three thousand promises from God for us in the New Testament. He is simply waiting for us to take Him up on His promises. Taking God up on one of His promises is a bit like showing up at the door of a friend who invited you over for coffee. The coffee has been promised to you but until you show up and take her up on it you are not able to enjoy its benefits! God is waiting for you and me to take Him up on His promises.

Recently I had to make a decision and I did not know what to do. I recalled a promise in James 1:5, "But if any of you lacks wisdom let him ask God, who gives generously to all without reproach, and it will be given to him."

"God, I really need wisdom on this," I begged. "Please show me what you want me to do as you promised you would through James." In time wisdom came. God does not answer every prayer immediately. While we are waiting He is still at work and often in the waiting He has something else to show us.

A promise from Isaiah has encouraged me this week as I've been down on myself: "Therefore the Lord longs to be gracious to you and therefore he exalts himself to show mercy to you. For the Lord is a God of justice; blessed are all those who wait for him" (Isaiah 30:18).

When I consider that God longs to show me compassion and graciousness I am overwhelmed and uplifted. I experience that He is indeed enough.

THE ENCOURAGEMENT OF OTHERS

We can't grow in our faith by ourselves. We need

the encouragement of others. Jesus himself needed close friends. He had the twelve disciples and of these He had three best buddies, Peter, James, and John. Although they let Him down, their mere friendship was an encouragement to Him. They had a hunger for truth. Why else would they leave all to follow Him?

There are different types of friendships. We all have acquaintances (a large group), we have good friends (a smaller group), and we have soul mates (the smallest group). All three are important. An acquaintance may be the gal in the office next to yours who doesn't know Christ. You are called to love her and pray for her to come to faith. A friend may be someone in your neighborhood with whom you walk. A soul mate should be a committed believer of the same sex with whom you can be completely honest. Together you laugh, cry, and challenge one another. She knows your fears and sins and sticks with you. You push each other to Jesus and encourage one another to be in His Word. You ask hard questions and encourage each other to do what is right, not what you feel like doing. Once I was sharing with my friend Anne about how irritated I was with my husband. It is so easy to get with women and bash husbands. After listening to my complaints she looked at me and simply said, "Susan what are you doing to move closer to him?" That's a good friend.

MENTORS

Another thing I pray for my children is that God will provide for them an older mentor who is a keen believer and who can encourage them, advise them, and share with them their life experiences. Every time they move to a new city I pray for God to provide a mentor for each of my sons and daughters and their spouses.

Our daughter Libby had five children in just under two years. Her eldest daughter was not yet two when she gave birth to quadruplets. She lives in Tennessee and I live in Virginia. It has been very hard to be so far away. Years ago I began to pray for a mentor for Libby. It took a few years but then God brought Leigh, an older mom and neighbor into her life. Leigh loves Christ and she loves my daughter. They meet regularly to pray, share, and simply talk. I am so grateful for Leigh.

My own mother was killed in a car crash at the age of eighty. The week before she died she and a small group of young girls had been gathered around her kitchen table in their regular study of the book of Romans. My mother-in-law lived to be ninety-seven. At the age of eighty-five she moved to a new city. She began mentoring twelve young mothers, some of whom did not yet have the assurance of Christ. Every Monday morning they gathered in her small retirement cottage where she taught them the Scriptures, starting in Genesis. She even gave them quizzes! For the next twelve years they met and once she took them and their husbands on a retreat. Whole families and yes, even a city, were impacted by an older woman who knew God's Word was the truth and was willing to share it with others.

Our son John had the privilege of being John Stott's study assistant for three years. Dr. Stott, a world famous scholar, author, and teacher had fourteen study assistants during his lifetime. He never married, but as a godly single man he has influenced countless young folks around the entire world. And his main message was lived out: "You can trust the word of God. "

You may come from a painful background; you may be married, single, widowed, or divorced. Whatever you come from, there is good news. God loves to do a new thing and you can be the first of a generation of families whose trust is in His Word. Your life can impact future generations for Christ.

When my husband John got his corneal transplant it was a new beginning. The old cornea had to be removed and a healthy one stitched in, which would enable him to see in a fresh new way. It took time for healing but the amazing clarity with which he began to see was remarkable. He saw in a way he never had before.

God's Word has the power to enable us to see life in a fresh new way. It has the power to change our lives, to give us the peace that we long for, and to enable us to see just how wide and long and high and deep is the love of Christ, and to know this love that surpasses knowledge that we may be filled to the measure of all the fullness of God.

> For this reason I bow my knees before the Father, from whom every family in heaven and on earth is named, that according to the riches of his glory he may grant you to be strengthened with power through his Spirit in your inner being so that Christ may dwell in your hearts through faith—that you, being rooted and grounded in love, may have strength to comprehend with all the saints what is

the breadth and length and height and depth and to know the love of Christ that surpasses knowledge, that you may be filled with all the fullness of God. (Ephesians 3: 14-18)

A TIME TO REFLECT:

1. Why is it important for me to have an authority in my life? How do I view Scripture? What role does it play in my life?

   Let's be honest here—If I have serious questions about the reliability of the Scriptures, am I willing to investigate, to study the works of scholars, to find answers to some of my questions? Am I avoiding Scripture because I don't like some of what it says? Am I simply lazy?

2. How might you identify with Billy Graham's struggle with the authority of the Scriptures? Is there a decision you need to make about your view of Scripture?

3. Do you know someone whose love of God's Word has genuinely impacted their life on a daily basis? What does this look like? What have you learned from observing this?

4. Do you know in your head the importance of God's Word but lack the desire to study it? God knows our hearts and He understands us. He knows how weak we are and He does not condemn us. He longs to speak to us through His word. We simply need to pray, "God give me a hunger to be in Your Word." And then take the first step—read a brief portion of it.

FOR FURTHER STUDY:

1. Turn to Luke chapter one.

    Background: Scholars agree that Luke was written by Luke himself, a physician and companion of Paul. Luke was a gentile Christian, well educated, wrote flawless Greek, and was well-versed in the culture of the Roman world. A.D. 60 is the best approximate date for the writing of this book. It is written to Theophilus, a wealthy citizen of Antioch who may or may not have been a believer. Luke was hopeful that Theophilus would distribute this letter widely.[3]

    Get some paper and a Bible. (It's fun to have fresh paper or a new journal and colored pens.) Pray for God to speak to you through His Word

2. Make three wide columns on your paper. Title the first column "verse," the second, "observation," and the third, "application."

    *   Read chapter one of Luke through one time.
    *   Go back to the beginning of the chapter and write out the first and second verses word by word under the verse column.
    *   In the observation column write down things you notice from verses one and two. In your observation, consider the questions: how, what, when, where, why, and ask yourself if there is a list of things here.
    *   Next move to the application column and ask yourself, "Is there anything here that applies to

my life now or might in the future?"

The goal here is not to get answers to every question but instead to give you tools to begin to dissect the Scripture on your own in order to find practical application for your life. It is both fun and helpful to do this together with a few others. God will show you different insights but you'll learn from each other. If you get stuck there are excellent commentaries to study.

Keep in mind: One of the great blessings in studying the Word is to let God speak directly to you. You do not have to be a scholar to hear His voice.

CHAPTER SIX

NATURAL GROWTH AND SPIRITUAL GROWTH: A NEW WAY OF LOOKING AT GROWTH

The vision in each of my eyes is not the same. One eye has an astigmatism and one doesn't. Although both eyes are very nearsighted, one is worse than the other. My ophthalmologist understands the differences in each eye and knows how to carefully craft different contacts or different glass lenses in order to correct my vision. Both eyes need to work in tandem for me to see optimally.

In the same way that my eyes are different and need to be treated differently, the way we grow naturally and spiritually are rather different.

Natural growth, as I am using the term, means growing from childhood into adulthood not just physically but intellectually and socially too. The goal of natural growth is to become a self-sufficient, thoughtful, and responsible human being. This is essential.

Spiritual growth however is rather different. Spiritual growth is our growth in relation to God, in faith, and into Christ likeness.

Too often we expect to grow in faith in the ways that

we grow in the natural areas. But spiritual growth is oh so different from natural growth. Understanding this difference in growth has greatly impacted my view of God. I call this a unique principle of juxtaposition. The dictionary defines juxtaposition (noun) as: "the juxtaposition of two contrasting objects, images, or ideas is the fact that they are placed together or described together, so that the differences between them are emphasized."[1]

Considering natural growth and spiritual growth side-by-side, similar to a juxtaposition, enables us to view life in a fresh yet contrasting way. Remember that one is not better than the other. They are merely different. Spiritual growth is not right and natural growth is not wrong. They are just different. And both are necessary. But, it is crucial to understand the differences in order to avoid frustration particularly as we attempt to grow in our faith.

Following are some examples of how this works.

1. *Natural growth involves becoming independent. However spiritual growth involves becoming more dependent.*

From the time our children are very young we teach them to become independent. We train them to go to the potty by themselves and then we cheer when they finally get it! We teach them how to make their own beds and clean up their own toys. We endure a lot of whining and "Do I have to do this, Mom?" Later we show them how to make a budget and teach them how to drive (albeit with fear and trembling)! We encourage them to take safe risks— try out for a team they might not make, take a class they may not do well in, make a friend who might reject them. We walk beside them in their disappointments but we are not afraid to let them fail. We encourage them to get back up and keep going. Our goal is to raise confident adults and growing in independence is crucial to the formation of their personal confidence. We are communicating: *I have confidence in you. You can do this.* A parent who does everything for her (or his) child has good intentions. She truly wants to help. But in the long run, he or she is actually undermining their child's confidence because the subtle message is: *You can't do this successfully so I will do it for you.* A parent who hovers over her child will be less likely to let go when she leaves home. This child will not be prepared for adulthood because she has not become independent from her parents. She will lack the personal confidence to handle life. Independence is a necessity for healthy natural growth.[2]

Spiritual growth on the other hand is completely different from natural growth. Spiritual maturity occurs when we become more dependent on God, not less.

As a young believer I tried so hard to trust God. I wanted to please Him. In a way I was determined to get this Christian life down, to complete one phase and move on to the next. It was as if I expected God to run along beside me cheering me on as I conquered different aspects of life. The harder I tried the more miserable I became. I stumbled and fell. What I needed was a Savior to carry and empower me, not a cheerleader to run beside me.

We expect to arrive at a place spiritually where we've learned "this," whatever the "this" is at the moment. Spiritually we long to arrive. We want to become independent spiritual adults. But we will never get there this side of heaven. Instead, as Jesus told His disciples, "Truly I say to you, unless you turn and become like children, you will never enter the kingdom of heaven" (Matt 18:3). A little child is completely dependent upon his parent.

What was happening to me and perhaps what happens to you is that we attempt to grow spiritually in the way we would naturally. But spiritual growth is just the opposite.

Recently I was very discouraged. There was an issue in my life that I was having a very hard time trusting God with. I was ashamed because I felt I should be able to trust Him by now. I'd known Christ for over forty-five years. I'd studied the Scriptures, been exposed to the teachings of great scholars, participated in small groups, and spoken and written myself. Yet I was struggling. While sharing with a close friend I exclaimed, "I should be able to trust God."

"Susan," she replied, "Who are you to think that you should be able to trust God?"

With that one statement she got me. I was leveled. I realized again I was merely a little child who couldn't even trust God. I needed His help to trust Him. It wasn't my ability, effort, or my background that mattered; it was my surrendering. I think two words God most loves to hear from us are "I can't."

When I come to the place of "I can't, but You can," I surrender my stubborn self sufficiency and once again become dependent upon Him. In doing so, I begin to see more glimpses of just how big He is.

Spiritual growth can stall if we interpret spiritual

maturity through the lenses of natural growth.

We might work hard to make something happen, think through every contingency, make plans, and then pray. When I was younger I used to get so put out when older saints would say, "All we can do is pray." I'd recoil and long to respond, "Do something!" But the older I get the more I realize prayer is the first, the continuing, and the follow up—not the last resort.

We must be alert to the danger of trying to grow spiritually in the way we grow naturally. It will only produce frustration. Spiritual growth is counter-intuitive and humbling.

Life says independence equals freedom; God says dependence upon Him equals freedom.

So if we want to mature spiritually, to experience a bigger God, then we have to become more dependent on Him, not less.

2. *Natural growth often means moving on to something else, something new but spiritual growth sometimes means to remain or to stay.*

"I've been there, done that. Now I'm moving on to the next thing."

Most likely each of us has felt this way at different times. It is good to move on. Our child needs to move on from his toddler bike to a two-wheeler. An older child must move on from easy classes to ones that really challenge her. Our adult child needs to move out of our home and into his own place even if it is tiny.

It's good to move on in our professions, or to change

professions and try something new. If we want to grow naturally we have to move on, otherwise we will become stagnant and perhaps depressed.

However if we apply this principle of natural growth to our spiritual growth we can get in trouble.

We had a friend who was a deeply committed believer. An entrepreneur, he quickly moved up the ranks in his profession. After each endeavor was successful he moved on to something else. His creativity and hunger to grow were inspiring. However this same way of thinking began to impact his spiritual life.

"I've been in Bible studies. I don't really need to do that anymore. I've been to church. I don't need to go anymore. I'm beyond that. I've read Christian books, now I'm ready to move on to books espousing other religions." He chose the wrong new things.

Slowly and subtly his relationship with the Lord began to wane. He made compromises in his life. Distancing himself from his believing friends, he adopted a theology different from orthodox Christianity. What happened? Many factors contributed but one was that he began to apply the principle of natural growth to spiritual growth. And he didn't even realize it.

While natural growth says we need to move on, to try new things, spiritual growth sometimes means remain or stay.

In the Bible, John 15 is known as the chapter on abiding. The Greek word for abide is *meno* and it has the connotation of dwell, continue, tarry, endure, remain. The English Standard Version translates it as "abide" and this word is used ten times in the first eleven verses. Christ himself says to us, "I am the vine; you are the branches. Whoever abides in me and I in him, he it is that bears much fruit, for apart from me you can do nothing" (John 15:5).

If we want to grow spiritually we need to remain in relationship with Jesus, to remain in fellowship with others, and to worship regularly with believers. Church is the one place we go purely to worship. It is the one place where we can be with people of every age, race, social, educational, and economic standing—the one place where we are all equal, all broken. No church is perfect. Just like the people who attend, they all have weaknesses. We need the fellowship of the weak and the broken on a regular basis. Remaining or abiding does not mean we shouldn't take on new endeavors to enhance our spiritual growth. A healthy, vital person pursues new opportunities while maintaining the basic disciplines of the spiritual life as their foundation.

Frustration occurs because I feel I've learned a basic spiritual principle. Now I want to learn something new. But the truth of the matter is that I continue to learn the same things over and over again in different situations. God is faithful. I am weak. His promises are true. Once again, I need to trust Him with this new issue.

So if we want to mature spiritually we dare not stray from the basic disciplines of spiritual growth: study of the Scriptures, prayer, fellowship, and worship. This often requires obedience, even when we don't feel like it.

3. *Natural growth involves complicating our lives, adding stuff to them. Spiritual growth can mean simplifying, laying things aside.*

We live in a culture with overwhelming options. Good options. It is far easier to make a wise choice when the option is between good and evil. But it can be overwhelming when the options all seem to be good ones. Making wise decisions is becoming more and more difficult and the multitude of choices is only going to increase for our children and grandchildren. The technological revolution has certainly contributed to this. It has both simplified our lives and complicated them.

Our lives and those of our children can become so packed that we find ourselves rushing from one event to the next as if we live on a merry-go-round that will not stop. Moms long for a snow day when school is canceled and everything stops for twenty-four hours! (Of course, if it goes on too long she becomes desperate for school to reopen!)

In the midst of so many options it is easy to fall prey to parental peer pressure. This happened to me. I was sitting in the stands of the local gym watching our twins, Susy and Libby, play basketball. As I watched I chatted with two other moms. One kept looking anxiously at her watch.

"I hope this game ends soon," she sighed. "My daughter has the lead role in the school musical and she has to practice. And she's the chair of the housing project her school is helping to renovate for a needy family."

"I know just how you feel," the other mom joined in. "My daughter is playing on the traveling basketball team so she has another practice after this one and she's the lead violinist in the orchestra which has a concert this weekend. She's also editor of the school paper and has deadlines."

Walking out of the gym that night I found myself thinking, *These two mothers are better mothers than I am. Their kids are involved in more worthwhile activities than mine are. I need to go home and sign my girls up for more things.* And then I realized I was falling to parental peer pressure—the pressure that says whoever's child is the most involved in activities is the best parent.

Wait a minute. We need to take a hard look at what we are doing. Do we want to sign our children up for one more activity that might win one more trophy—a trophy that ten years from now will be gathering dust on a closet shelf—or do we want to say no to another activity and instead set aside several nights a week to have family dinner together in order to build family friendships? Ten years from now which will be more important, siblings who are friends or trophies covered with dust?

Some of us need to simplify our natural lives and some of us need to branch out. You may have a reticent child who needs to be pushed to participate in an activity. You may need to take advantage of good options yourself. Our needs will be influenced by our personalities, our geographical location, and the needs of those around us. Either way if our decision involves a child, don't expect them to respond positively. They may pitch a fit. Our job as parents is to make a wise decision with the long-term view in mind.

This particular example of natural growth has both positive and negative aspects. We need God's wisdom to discern what is right for us and for our families. And that decision will be different in each season of life. And different for each family.

While natural growth may mean adding things to your life or in some cases learning to say no, spiritual growth often means simplifying.

Both my mother and my mother-in-law were godly women. Frequently when I was frustrated or worried about something one of them would say to me, "Susan, You just have to trust in the Lord." Often this made me want to scream! I wanted action not simple faith. When I sit with older men and women I notice they have learned what really matters. Years of acquiring biblical knowledge, walking through blessing and tragedy yet experiencing God's faithfulness—no matter what—has simplified their faith. They have learned to let go of many things. And in their letting go they have come to a resting place, relying on Him. Simplification has released the fresh air of freedom.

My friend Ann is critically ill. After five years of stage three-c cancer and four rounds of chemotherapy, she still has cancer cells in her body. While her body is declining her spirit is soaring. This week she shared this experience:

Yesterday I took a walk on the path in the stream valley park near my home. The brilliant sunshine made everything shimmer. Beside the path was a small pool of water. I paused to admire the vivid pattern of leaves lining the bottom of this pool. Various hues of brown, amazing lines—it was as if I were seeing with new eyes the extraordinary beauty of a puddle I passed by frequently. Then I noticed, superimposed on the brown leaves, the reflection of towering trees against a blazing blue sky. A slight breeze stirred the surface of the water, obscuring the view of the leaf-lined bottom. All I could see was the brilliant, perfect reflection of the trees and sky.

The gift cancer has given me is the eyes to see the beauty of this life, a mottled design, superimposed by a vision of the next world, in its purity, light, and glory. The times of sadness, stress, and grief come like the wind on the surface of the pool. My view of the next life comes into sharper focus.

"For now we see in a mirror dimly, but then face to face. Now I know in part; then I shall know fully, even as I have been fully known. So now faith, hope, and love abide, these three; but the greatest of these is love" (1 Corinthians 13:12-13).

While natural growth often means adding to our life, spiritual growth will sift things out causing us to value simplicity.

4. *Natural growth encourages fast results and denigrates waiting. Spiritual growth insists that we learn to wait on the Lord.*

There's a TV commercial currently running which shows an attractive, adult man seated around a table with some young children about the age of five. He's chatting with them about why his latest smart phone is the best. "What do you like the most kids—big or little?" "Big," they all chime in. "What do you like the most, fast or slow?" "Fast," they quickly respond.

"So big and fast are best?" He asks. "Yes" they all shout and he proceeds to explain his latest hi-tech product, which is both big (in its capacity not size) and fast and therefore the best.

In natural life fast can be a good thing. Being on the fast track in your career has many advantages. Learning to read at age four does bring joy for the child and peace for the parents! However, fast is not always best even in our natural lives. Many musicians, actors, and sports heroes become celebrities in their youth only to fall into miseries of all kinds because fame came before they were mature enough to handle it.

We live in an on-demand culture. We have grown accustom to instant everything. Subtly, our expectation—our demand—has become "I should not have to wait."

Hold on. A lot of life is waiting.

We have to wait to find a job, to earn a promotion, to learn the medical test results, to be reconciled with someone, to find a mate, to get out of debt, to be healed, etc. A lot of life is waiting. We do our children a great disservice if we don't teach them how to wait when they are small. This is counter-cultural. If we train that young child to wait his turn to play with a toy, to wait until he's earned the money to buy a bike, to wait to get a smart phone, or a car, or to date, then our child will be better equipped to wait as an adult. He will be more likely to wait for sexual satisfaction until marriage, to wait to earn a promotion legally rather than resorting to white collar or blue collar crime to get there faster, to wait for a marriage to be healed rather than rushing to the divorce court. A lot of life is waiting and we don't like it.

Learning to wait in the natural realm will make it easier to practice the discipline of waiting in our spiritual growth. God is not in a hurry. He does what is best not what is fast.

The prophet Isaiah depicts God saying, "My thoughts are not your thoughts and neither are your ways my ways, as the heavens are higher than the earth, so are my ways higher than your ways and my thoughts than your thoughts" (Isaiah 55: 8-9). David encourages us, "Wait for the Lord; be strong, and let your heart take courage; wait for the Lord!" (Psalm 27:14).

Waiting is no fun. It is frustrating when we pray and pray and don't feel like we get any answers. It's even more painful for a parent when her child prays and prays about something and finally says, "God hasn't answered my prayer. He doesn't care."

Oh, but He does. I have found that God answers prayer in three basic ways. He answers yes, no, or wait. But He always answers out of His perfect love. When He answers no consider it a love-no. He loves you and your child or your friend with perfect love. He may be protecting you from something that is not the best for you or your child. He alone has the whole picture and He alone knows the future. Silence may indicate that His answer is wait. It helps to remember God is working while we are waiting.

Thomas Merton was a mentor to James Finley. Finley relates a time in which Merton told him to quit trying so hard in prayer. He said to him,

> How does an apple ripen? It just sits in the sun.
> A small green apple cannot ripen in one night by

tightening all its muscles, squinting its eyes, and tightening its jaw in order to find itself the next morning miraculously large, red, ripe, and juicy beside its small green counterparts. Like the birth of a baby or the opening of a rose, the birth of true self takes place in God's time. We must wait for God, we must be awake, we must trust in his hidden action within us.[3]

On a dark, dreary winter day I see no evidence of spring. It is hidden. Everything just feels gray. And sometimes it seems to go on forever. But underneath all the dreariness, growth, beautiful growth, is taking place. Seeds lying dormant are being nurtured until the time is right for them to burst forth in color shouting, "Spring is here!" If the fragile plants burst out too early they risk being damaged by a late frost. Timing is crucial. God's gift of creation gives us many insights with which to understand His ways of working in our lives.

Waiting is a normal part of both our natural life and our spiritual life. Learning to wait in our natural lives will make it easier for us when we have to wait on God.

5. *Natural growth promotes working harder. Spiritual growth calls for rest and worship.*

24-7 is most often a positive statement. A store is never closed. There is always complete access, on-going availability. Technology never sleeps nor rests. Information is current 24-7. Google doesn't take a nap! The message is we are working harder than ever. And so we are the best.

A hard worker is a person to be admired whereas one who rests might be considered lazy or at least, less respected. There is nothing wrong with hard work. It is to be valued. But sometimes we can over do it.

Washington DC is a city of over-achievers and accomplished multi-taskers. In our city, significance has become an idol. And stress has become a status symbol. Whoever is the most stressed is obviously the most significant. We race around from one event to another, one carpool to the next. We complain to our friend about all that is on our calendar for the week. Sundays are no exception. Few today remember when stores were closed on Sundays and there were no sporting events. Life took a break and families spent time at church and lingered over a big meal. With the values of today, that would seem like such a waste.

Our view of hard work impacts how we raise our kids. We have to train them to work hard, to do their best.

Our son John had an easy time academically in high school. He was making all A's with a few B's. But what was concerning to me and to my husband was the fact that he was not working; he even appeared to be a bit lazy. We wanted him to learn the value of hard work. After much discussion and prayer we sat down with him together.

"Son," my husband said, "God has given you the gift of a sharp brain. We don't feel you are developing the discipline of using it as you could, so this semester we are going to impose a study hall each evening where you will spend two hours studying. If you've finished your homework you can read a book related to your studies. We believe that you can make all A's. "

Our son was not happy with us, however study hall commenced and he did make straight A's. But more importantly he learned the value of hard work. And he learned personal discipline. Thankfully he was the only one of our five kids who needed this particular discipline strategy.

In the midst of teaching our kids the value of hard work we have to take care that we not become encore parents. An encore parent is one for whom nothing is ever good enough. You son scores six points in a basketball game and you quickly come up with a game plan so he will score more next time. Or you daughter makes the chorus in the school musical and you push her to try for a solo part. This may not be wrong, but sometimes we need to merely stop and celebrate the accomplishment that has been achieved. If we are always looking for more—for an encore—our children can feel that no matter what they do it is never going to be enough. As an adult you may still be trying to please a parent or a spouse. You may still feel that no matter what you do it isn't enough. The person you are trying to please is never satisfied. He or she still wants an encore. And that person might be you.

Working harder can lead to greater accomplishments and this is good. However we have to take care that our identity and that of our children is not determined by what we accomplish. Accomplishment can become an idol. Our value should not be determined by what we accomplish but by who we belong to.

I grew up in a home with a dad who was both verbally and physically affectionate. I remember curling up in his lap and hearing him say, "Susan I love you so much."

"Why?" I asked. "Just because you are mine," he replied.

God loves each one of us just because we are His, not because of our hard work or our accomplishments. Certainly hard work and discipline are essential in order to fulfill God's purposes in our lives. But it's easy for us to put too much emphasis on our efforts. Because of this He created the Sabbath. He knows we need a day of worship—of focusing on Him and rest. We cannot grow in a healthy way without rest. We will simply burn out.

Resting is a discipline that reminds us God can handle things for a day if we just pull back and quit. Isn't it ridiculous to even say that? I have to laugh at myself for this way of thinking shows just how much I think God needs me, how crucial I am. Actually He doesn't. Recognizing this is humbling but freeing. God doesn't need me nearly as much as He loves me. He knows how desperately I need to let Him take over.

Our spiritual growth will stall if we do not take time for a Sabbath.

The challenge for each of us is to develop a vision for a Sabbath day for ourselves and for our families. What would a real day of rest and worship look like for us? What can we do to focus on God and to worship Him? What changes do we need to make to insure both emotional and physical rest at this season of life? How can we find "Sabbath moments" throughout the week?

In natural growth we learn to value hard work yet spiritual growth enables us to view our accomplishments from His perspective. Our human frailty calls for rest and our heart cries out to worship a God who is so much bigger than any accomplishment. In a Sabbath rest we relinquish control to Him. This enables us to step back and see Him in His vastness. David describes it this way, "Be still and know that I am God" (Psalm 46:10).

> 6. *Natural growth might say don't impose on that person again; whereas in spiritual growth, God says "Call on me more!"*

We feel badly when we have to impose on a friend for a favor, especially if we've already asked her for something recently. A carpool pick up, a ride to the airport, another job reference, help with a project. Most of us don't want to burden others. We'd rather do it ourselves. We don't want to acquire the reputation of being a needy person. Instead we think it's best to be the one who cares for others.

It has been said that there are generally two kinds of people. One walks into the room with a "here I am" attitude. Somebody please reach out to me. The other walks in with a "there you are" spirit. How can I care for you? We want to be "there you are" people and we want to raise "there you are" kids. This is not our normal instinct. We are self-centered. We would all rather be cared for. It has to be cultivated in our own lives and in the lives of our kids and grandkids. We cultivate a "there you are spirit" in many small ways. Ask your child, "Is there a lonely kid in your class? Could you ask her to eat lunch with you today?" Is there a neighbor who needs her yard mowed for free?

In our natural lives we take care that we don't over-burden others. However spiritually, we can never over-burden God!

Too often my response to God is: *I can't go to Him*

again for that, I'm too embarrassed, I've let Him down. He's already done so much. I don't want to be piggy. He must be weary of hearing my cries.

But He is saying to you and to me, "Call on me."

The psalmist puts it this way, "What shall I render to the Lord for all his benefits to me? I will lift up the cup of salvation and call on the name of the Lord" (Psalm 116: 12).

How counterintuitive. I would have answered "I'll repay His goodness by trying to be better, working harder, sinning less." Wrong answer. He simply wants me to call on Him with a thankful heart, once again expressing dependence upon him.

We call on Him not because of who we are but because of who He is—the King of kings, the Lord of lords, our Savior, and our Father. _

Natural growth cautions us from burdening others too much; however in spiritual growth our Father God exclaims, "Call on me more!"

7. Natural growth wants to live. In spiritual growth we must learn to die.

To grow naturally we must take care of ourselves. A healthy diet, exercise, rest, a sense of purpose, all contribute to a long life. We want to live, to enjoy God's creation, to experience the plan He has for us! Natural growth is good! But in spiritual growth we must learn to die to ourselves.

One of my biggest frustrations in my spiritual growth comes because I don't want to call on Him. I want to do "it"—whatever the "it" is—myself. I want to be independent. So I try to trust, to believe, to be good, to do the right thing, and most often I fail miserably. Like a child I say, *I can do this myself.* Then I realize I am using the principle of natural growth to try to mature spiritually. And once again I have to come to the place where I fall on my knees and say to Him, *I can't Lord. I want you to do this within me.* I have to die to my own efforts. Once again I have to become dependent upon Him rather than independent, relying on my own efforts.

The ultimate juxtaposition is that in the end we do get to live. Because Jesus died in our place. His death on the cross was so that we might not remain dead but that in physical death we might be transported into eternal life.

In natural life we strive to live to the fullest. Yet in our spiritual life we live to die for an even better life—shedding a weak body hampered by human frailty, to acquire an eternal body with no sin, made perfect by His resurrection power.

He died that we might live and when we die we will live forever with Him!

Sometimes I get my contacts mixed up. I put the wrong lens in the wrong eye. That's uncomfortable. I can't see properly and my vision is limited. My focus is messed up and I miss out on the richness that clear vision provides. I have to put the right contact in the correct eye in order to be able to see clearly.

In a similar way we need to take care that we do not get our lenses of natural and spiritual growth mixed up. Both are necessary yet different. If I see spiritual growth through the lenses of natural growth it is going to mess up my focus. There is so much more going on than what we see.

When the eyes of our hearts are used correctly we will be able to see with a greater clarity the hope to which He has called us, the riches of His glorious inheritance in His holy people, and His incomparably great power for us who believe (paraphrased from Ephesians 1:18-19).

"I am the resurrection and the life. Whoever believes in me, though he die, yet shall he live, and everyone who lives and believes in me shall never die" (Jesus in John 11:25-26).

A TIME TO REFLECT

1. Natural growth and spiritual growth as presented here are two different things. How would you explain the difference?
2. Which juxtaposition did you find most enlightening for your life at this moment? Why?
3. Do you know someone older than you are who has a vital relationship with the Lord? In what ways have you witnessed their dependence on the Lord?
4. God is always working even while we are waiting. What are some lessons you have learned in times of waiting? What comforts you when you are in a time of waiting? What Scriptures are helpful to you?

FOR FURTHER STUDY:

1. Read Luke chapter one. Write down everything you learn about Elizabeth and Zechariah. Use commentaries to further your own findings.
2. Consider the theme of waiting in their lives. Elizabeth struggled with infertility. Was her behavior the reason for her infertility? (Hint: see Luke 1:6.) Why do you suppose they had to wait all these years to have a child? There is not one correct answer so use your imagination and anything you learn from commentaries. What do you learn about waiting that encourages you?

3. In this chapter we discussed seven juxtapositions. What other ones would you add that distinguish between natural growth and spiritual growth? How is this helpful to you?

Chapter Seven

Perspective—The Importance of Seeing Beyond Your Own

We have a little farm in the Shenandoah Mountains of Virginia. It is nestled in the hills right beside the Appalachian Trail. I love to hike a portion of the trail that winds its way up a woodsy hill across from our pasture. After climbing for about twenty minutes, the forest opens up into a large field. In the midst of the field there's a very old apple tree that seems to preside over the surrounding hills and valleys. Right under the apple tree is a weathered bench where many a hiker has taken a rest and contemplated the amazing scenery.

Recently I started my hike on a chilly, wet day. The fog was so thick that I couldn't see more than a few feet in front of me. The trees were shrouded in a blanket with only those closest clearly discernible. Because I couldn't see very far I noticed details I often missed—vapor collecting in little pellets on a large branch, a variety of different types of bark decorating trees in my immediate path, a bird nearby calling out a love song to His creator, the sound of a branch breaking beneath my feet. In a sense, I enjoyed my restricted vision. But it was limited to just what was in front of me. And the further I went I found myself longing for a bigger view, for more clarity. As I got closer to the crest of the hill, the fog began to lift. When I emerged from the woods and stepped into the large pasture, I was blinded by the blazing sun and a grand, clear view of surrounding mountains on every side. Suddenly a whole new vista opened up to me. It was startling in its vastness and its diversity. Now I could see for miles and miles. The myopic vision I had on the foggy trail gave way to a large view of so many things I had missed in the fog. My perspective was enhanced and magnified.

It's easy for our view of God to become like my limited vision in the fog. If we rely solely on our own eyes to see God, our view of Him will be severely restricted. But our vision of Him can be enlarged when we see him from the perspective of others. The same principle is true in life. Our worldview grows and our vision of God grows as we encounter different places, peoples, and experiences. There are many ways to do this but here are four:

1. EXPOSE YOURSELF TO THE PERSPECTIVE OF OTHERS

Recently I rode a bus from Memphis, Tennessee to Nashville, Tennessee. It was such an unusual four-hour trip that I emailed my kids the following:

> When I got on a very crowded bus this morning I found myself a minority person sitting next to my soon-to-be new best friend, Ida Mae, a woman from the deep South. She had gotten up at 3:00 am to get

on her first bus of what was to be a thirty-hour trip for her. As we hit the road, she and I began reading our Bibles. Hers was a big one zipped in a case made by her grandkids and stuffed with old letters and bills. She fell asleep in the midst of reading but would awaken every now and then to chat with me. At sixty she's the eldest of twenty-one children. Her mother had sixty-six grandchildren and one hundred and four great grandchildren when she died at seventy-six years old. "I has ten kids myself. I had five with my husband then he left and I had five more. My life was a mess so I decided I needed to go to church and I got saved. My life done changed. My husband, he left his next wife and wanted me to shack up again with him but I told him I don't do that shacking no more. Jesus got me. My daddy was a railroad man and I cleaned hotels. One of my brothers died last year and he never been out of his neighborhood his whole life. I finished eighth grade."

We had a ten-minute stop in Jackson, Tennessee so I got off to get some coffee from the vending machine. I found one machine that said twenty-five cents a cup. "Is this for real?" I asked another customer. He replied, "Where are YOU from?" It was for real so I got two cups for fifty cents! Back on the bus I began to freeze so I tore up my newspaper and stuffed it into the air vents to block the air. Ida Mae woke up again and she had a light blanket that she took off and said to me, "You wrap up in it: I don need it. I got sleeves." I had sleeves too, but she took care of me.

My bus trip brought laughter and tears to my eyes. It also made me realize again how the world we live in is often small. We are without perspective and sadly insulated, so protected in our particular circles. It is important to get out of our closeted comfort zones. I long for my grandchildren to have different life experiences like my bus ride and to spend time with people unlike themselves. It will enlarge their perspective on life and give them a much bigger picture of how big God is.

Unlike Ida Mae, my friend Bill has traveled the world. I asked him how exposure to different people had broadened his perspective:

> Once when I was in India I was standing in a long line at a train station. I was very stressed because I was afraid I was going to miss the train. When I got to the ticket counter with the exact cost of the ticket, the attendee, noticing I was an American, demanded more money. I refused to pay the bribe and just simply stood there. I felt powerless, devalued, and angry. I was used to being in a position of control. But then it dawned on me that most folks in the world exist in a state of powerlessness. Most feel devalued, hopeless. It opened my eyes to a greater realization of how limited my perspective is and how spoiled I am and how blessed I am.

Spending time with people unlike ourselves will not only enlarge our view of God's world, but also make us more open to the amazing ways in which He is working that we do not often see in our day-to-day lives. It is wise parents who are intentional in exposing their children to people unlike themselves. Invite people from other countries into your home. Ask them to tell their story. Insist your kids be present. If they are teens they will likely roll their eyes and say, "Do I have to?" Simply respond, "Yes, this is a family event." They may not appreciate these stories now but God will use them to enrich their lives. Entertain young adults who have a vital faith. Have them share their testimonies. Your kids will look up to them and be more interested in anything they say than you say. Think "exposure" as you raise your children.

It doesn't matter if you are married or single or have kids, still think "exposure," especially when you are in a hard place. Get together with someone whose life experience is different than yours. Ask them to tell their story. Everyone has a story they want to tell. In hearing someone else's story our perspective will be enlarged and our current issues will be seen from a healthier perspective.

Our vision of God is enlarged when we view His people and His creation through different lenses.

2. CONSIDER HIS PERSPECTIVE

Have you ever found yourself thinking: *No one knows, no one cares, no one really understands, no one appreciates how hard this (whatever the issue of the moment) is for me.*

Sometimes we blame our spouse because he or she doesn't understand, our friend because she is not responding in the way I need her to, my boss because he doesn't appreciate me, my parents or in-laws who don't know how hard my life is.

It is good to ask, "Am I looking to the wrong people in the wrong places to meet my needs? Perhaps I should be looking to Christ."

Where in His life did He experience what I am experiencing? Is it possible He might know exactly how I am feeling? That He might actually understand my raw emotions?

Two passages in the Bible have had a radical impact on my life. They have enabled me to consider my issues from the perspective of Jesus.

"Therefore he had to be made like his brothers in every respect, so that he might become a merciful and faithful high priest in the service of God, to make propitiation for the sins of the people. For because he himself has suffered when tempted, he is able to help those who are being tempted" (Hebrews 2:17-18).

"Since then we have a great high priest who has passed through the heavens, Jesus the Son of God, let us hold fast our confessions. For we do not have a high priest who is unable to sympathize with our weaknesses, but one who in every respect has been tempted as we are yet without sin. Let us then with confidence draw near to the throne of grace, that we may receive mercy and find grace to help in time of need" (Hebrews 4:14-16).

What does this mean and how does this work out in everyday life?

Simply put it means that anything I am feeling or experiencing, Jesus Himself has already experienced, but without sin. He knows how I feel. He understands my challenge in a way that no other human being can.

Here are some examples:

The agony of a difficult decision.

Perhaps you are facing the agony of a difficult decision. All day long, even when you are doing routine tasks, it is on your mind. Its weight is heavy, tiresome, and frightening. Clarity seems illusive. You feel scared and lonely. In the moment it's easy to think, *No one knows how I feel; no one understands the agony in my heart.*

But there is one who does.

Picture Jesus in the garden of Gethsemane (in Matthew 26). Utterly alone, He asked His Father three times if there was any way the cup (the crucifixion) could be taken away from Him. Imagine Him wrestling with this decision. Could He go through with it? Was there no other way? It must have been agony.

The pain of betrayal.

Have you ever been betrayed by a friend? A friend with whom you have shared deep secrets in confidence has told someone else. A colleague you have trusted has taken advantage of you. A spouse has walked out on you. A child has turned against you. Shocked, angry, and deeply wounded, your heart has been pierced. How will you ever trust again?

Surely no one can understand how deeply this hurt has penetrated, how utterly devastated I am.

But Jesus does.

Remember His disciple Peter, the one he called the rock on whom He was going to build His church? When things got difficult, Peter denied three times that he even knew Jesus let alone was one of His dearest friends. How do you think Jesus felt? And then in the garden (Matthew 26). Jesus asked His three best friends, Peter, James, and John, to be with Him, to stay with Him, to pray with Him. And they fell asleep. Didn't they understand how much He needed them? They let Him down. Betrayal and loneliness must have been crushing to Jesus as a man.

The pain of singleness.

I have many single friends of varying ages. Some are single again and some have never married. Many are enjoying their singleness and understand it is a calling, even a gift. Paul himself considered singleness as a gift and a calling. Jesus implied the same thing (1 Corinthians 7:7, Matthew 19:11). One of our heroes in the faith, John Stott, remained single for ninety years. Twice in his young years he thought he would marry but each time he lacked the assurance to move forward and as time passed he embraced the gift of being single as God's call for him. His singleness gave him the freedom to accomplish far more than he would have been able to do with a family.

Most who are single would admit they have at different times struggled with their singleness. It can be lonely. There is not one person to whom you are the most important person. With our cultural focus on marriage and family, it is easy to feel left out, less than, even undesired. And it can be humiliating if someone assumes you are lesbian or gay simply because you are single. There is great pain in being misunderstood. It's easy to wonder, *Does anyone really understand how I feel?*

Yes, Jesus does.

He too was single. And He was single in a culture and time when the expectation was to marry. Although the early prophet Jeremiah was told by Yahweh not to marry (Jeremiah 16:1-4), most scholars say the idea of celibacy was foreign to Judaism. Palestinian teacher Simeon ben Azzai (2nd century CE) was a rare exception. Remaining single, he claimed that his love of the Torah prevented him from being a proper husband to a human wife.[1] However he preached the duty of procreation for others. During the time of Jesus, a small group of Jews, the Essenes, practiced celibacy. Yet in Jesus' day, it would have been very unusual to be unmarried and both He and His cousin John the Baptist remained single. So He was likely considered weird in His day.[2]

We can assume Jesus was tempted sexually. This may horrify you but if He was tempted in every way that we have been yet without sin, that includes all sexual temptations—those toward the opposite sex or the same sex. He understands the agony of every temptation—to satisfy sexual desires, to give into the power of addictions, etc. He endured forty straight days of being tempted. Yes, He knows how utterly miserable it is to go through a season of temptation. Yet in every temptation He resisted. He chose celibacy, which is sexual purity for a single person. He chose God's will over Satan's enticements.

In the midst of the agony of temptation Paul reminds us, "No temptation has overtaken you that is not common to man. God is faithful, and he will not let you be tempted beyond your ability, but with the temptation he will also provide the way of escape, that you may be able to endure it" (1 Corinthians 10:13). God always gives us the power to resist temptation when we turn to Him.

The pain of failing as a parent.

If you are a parent with young children you have already experienced failure. Each one of us struggles as we try to raise our kids. You may wonder, *Have I ruined my child for life?* Or your child may have run away. You may not even know where she is. An adult child may have completely cut off his relationship with you. The ache of your loss and your feelings of guilt as a parent scream condemnation and explode with heartache. Your wounds and regrets run deep, deeper hurts than anyone else could possibly understand.

But, Jesus does.

Although He had no biological children, His disciples became His family, His children. He spent three years of his life teaching, training and above all loving them. Yet they still displayed sibling rivalry! They argued about who was the greatest among them. James and John even went so far as to ask Jesus if they (not the others) could have the best position in his glory. Even their mom got in on this request (from Mark 9 & 10, Matthew 20). Jesus had to deal with pushy moms! It is almost funny. And then there was Judas. Even though He spent approximately the same number of years with Jesus as the other eleven, he eventually betrayed Him. Jesus Himself had a prodigal. He, the perfect "parent," the only one with no sin, understands your pain. You can take comfort that He understands but there's more.

Because of His death on the cross for our sins and

for those of our children, and especially because of His power which not even death could limit, you can have the assurance that your ability to ruin your child is not nearly as great as His power to redeem your child.

The pain of waiting.

So much of life is waiting. And we don't like it. We wait for a job, a relationship to be healed, a spouse, a promotion. We wait to be vindicated, for a child to learn discipline, for a cure for cancer, and our list goes on. As we saw in the previous chapter, culture says we deserve fast, instant, immediate. This is an illusion. Living in a culture that promotes fast makes waiting even harder. And sometimes in the weariness of waiting we wonder if God has forgotten us. *Will this ever end? What is the purpose of all this waiting? Is there anyone who understands my exhaustion, or feels my loss of hope?*

Yes, once again Jesus does.

I wonder if He ever got frustrated at having to wait thirty years to begin His public ministry. And then to have just three years to complete it? In terms of modern day strategic planning this is a poor way to change the world. It helps to remember that in the waiting God was bringing together many things so that in "the fullness of time" His ministry could begin. When we experience the frustration of waiting, it helps to remember while we are waiting God is working. And we can be comforted by the fact that His Son Jesus had to wait too.

Not too long after I began this practice of asking where in Christ's life He experienced what I am experiencing. I had the opportunity to apply this to my life in two unusual ways.

Feeling falsely accused, dirty.

My husband was serving as the senior minister of a large church in the Washington DC area. Unbeknownst to him, a man on our staff had engaged in improper behavior with some women in our church. When the situation became public the press jumped on it. I remember driving in the car with my five young children when the all-news network on the radio broke in with the lead, "Sex scandal at local church." The reporter went on to name my husband as the senior leader of the church and to briefly describe some of the details, not all of which were accurate. Although I knew what had happened, I was humiliated for my young children to have to hear their dad's name on national radio and I was furious that he was being falsely accused in his handling of this awful incident. My husband had not done anything wrong. He was however the top man in charge and thus was held responsible. I understood that mentality. But what surprised me the most was how it made me feel. I felt dirty. I had not done anything wrong. Yet I felt dirty simply from being so closely associated with what had happened. I did not like feeling dirty. It wasn't fair. I wasn't guilty. And then I remembered the Hebrews passages. *This one is tough,* I mused. *Where in Jesus' life did He experience this feeling of dirty, this feeling of shame?*

The answer hit me like a ton of bricks. Jesus was pure. Perfect purity, without any sin, any dirt (2 Corinthians 5:21). I, on the other hand, was sinful. I was dirty. As painful as it was for me, who in my sin nature was full of dirt, imagine how much more painful it must have been for Jesus to have to take my dirt, my shame, my sin on His pure shoulders to the cross. What a shocking pain that must have been for a pure savior. I had never appreciated before the emotional pain my sin caused Him. Yes, He understood how painful it was to feel dirty in a far more profound way than I could ever imagine.

The sadness of the empty nest—really?

I grew up in a large family and married into one as well. Christmases were always crowded, loud, happy occasions. In fact, I had never experienced a Christmas without lots of family around until several years ago. Our three eldest children were already married and then our twins, Susy and Libby, got married the same summer—six weeks apart. It just so happened that the upcoming Christmas each of our kids planned to be with their in-law families. For the first time in my entire life I faced the holidays alone. An acquaintance said to me, "Susan, this can be a special time for you and John, a sweet couple time together." I laughingly replied, "Do you know what my husband does? He's a pastor and Christmas is a really busy time for him." He, like most ministers, is rarely home during this season. He is overwhelmed with parishioners whose lives seem to fall apart during the holidays. He is stressed about sermons he is preparing. In fact most likely he will be grumpy. No, it's not realistic to imagine cuddling up together to roast chestnuts by an open fire!

As Christmas approached I prepared myself. Because we are a large church we have several services on Christmas Eve. I knew John would be gone from about 3:00 pm until 1:00 am. Friends invited me over but I felt I wanted to be alone with the Lord, so after going to a service I curled up all alone on the couch with my Bible in front of the Christmas tree. Once again I turned to Hebrews. *My nest is really empty now Lord. I feel deserted. I feel sad. I am lonely. I know it says in Hebrews that you have experienced everything thing that I have but how could you relate to my empty nest? You didn't even have kids.* And then I began to imagine what it was like for God on Christmas Eve. His Christmas Eve couldn't have been more opposite than mine. He was sending His only Son with whom He had created the earth (Genesis 1:26), with whom He had enjoyed 24/7 fellowship for all eternity, and from whom He had never been separated, to come to earth as God-made-man. He was sending Him to be born in a dirty stable, persecuted, misunderstood, verbally abused, physically beaten, and finally murdered on a cross to take on my sins just because the Father loved me. In emptying my nest, I sent my children off to good things, not off to a death—a death that was underserved but a death that was to save my life and yours. That quiet evening I had a glimpse into the pain of our Father God "emptying His nest." Still today I view Christmas Eve from a very different perspective. His cost. His astounding love. He alone understands my feelings, even my empty nest.

Some of these illustrations may appear to be farfetched. Yet in creating us with an imagination, God has given us a means whereby we can enter in to His story. We are able to imagine how He (in his humanity) felt in various situations. In entering into His story we are drawn into a more intimate relationship with Him. And this enables us to appreciate to a greater degree the bigness and complexity of His character and of His love.

Psychiatrist and author Curt Thompson puts it like this: "What if emotion, as we understand it, is a reflection of what God experiences in his heart? Wouldn't we do well to attend to this aspect of our minds since doing so would mean paying attention to a part of us that reflects God's being (albeit ours is a less intense version?)."[3]

There are many more examples waiting for you and me to discover. What issue is causing you angst at this moment? What feelings are you struggling with? Ask God to lead you to a time in His Son's life when He experienced the same feelings. He is the only one who truly understands how you feel. He is the one who can provide deep supernatural comfort. The writer of the Hebrews reminds us, "Let us then *with confidence* draw near to the throne of grace, that we may receive mercy and find grace to help in time of need" (Hebrews 4:16, emphasis mine).

3. CULTIVATE YOUR IMAGINATION

One of the most precious things about being created in the image of God is that we possess some of His character. A part of His character is His imagination. What imagination it took for Him to create His creatures and His world! He has given us this precious trait. I could not have come up with the examples above if it were not for this gift.

Use imagination to nurture the "power of wonder."

I love to watch a toddler discover something new. I remember when Susy was about four and she saw the ocean for the first time. Her blue eyes widened in amazement as she exclaimed, "Mommy, it is too full. You need to let some of it out." Often as we grow older we lose our ability to marvel and wonder at God's creation. Our tendency is to take for granted, to overlook, to miss the detail, the sweet hidden message.

Pope John Paul II encouraged us, "I am convinced that this is how beauty works: while no human experience can disclose what the mystery of God is, experiences that brim with beauty (or point poignantly to beauty's absence) can suddenly make us aware of the enticing mystery enveloping us. We are caught in its midst, and wonder is the only appropriate attitude."[4]

Some of you are gifted artists, musicians, poets, writers, philosophers, sculptors, or filmmakers. Consider that God has given you this gift so that as you develop it and share it, you can enlarge not only your own view of God but someone else's view of God as well.

Philosopher Chris Yates says it this way, "The imagination amounts to a special intuitive, and indeed sometimes deliberate, stock of wonder, and creative attention in each of us. It allows us to seek and grasp those truths that tend to stand beyond our more logical and fact-minded modes of cognition, and is often a crucial means by which we engage with moments of profound beauty."

Use imagination to experience a richness of worship.

Our Sunday morning worship service begins with the congregation on our feet, singing hymns of praise. Standing beside others with my eyes closed I'm lifted out of myself into another realm. Sometimes I imagine myself on the Sea of Galilee surrounded by believers of all races united in worship of Jesus. Music enhances my worship.

When we attend concerts and listen to music in our home or car we just might find ourselves lifted out of our own surroundings into a new realm of worship which carries us beyond the confines of our own faith and enlarges our view of our creator God.

Guard your imagination.

Our imagination, like many gifts, can be used for good or for evil. We imagine someone doesn't like us because she did not respond to an email or text or she failed to talk to us when we saw her. We imagine an illness, an enemy, a criticism. Imagination gone astray can lead to the development of heresy, a new religion, an ill-conceived philosophy, or depression. We must take care to guard our imaginations and test it against the truth contained in God's Word, our ultimate authority. If our imaginations lead to the creation of something that is in any way contrary to the Word of God or dishonoring to Him, it is inspired by the enemy not by the Holy Spirit, and we must delete it immediately.

In this world we will have trouble. We will suffer. Yet in this suffering there is redemption. We are able to identify in part with the sufferings of Jesus. No other religious leader in the world, not Gandhi, not Mohammed, not Buddha, not Confucius, or any other one was a *suffering* Savior. We have the opportunity to use our imaginations in order to better understand our Savior's identification with us in our suffering. He gets us. When we understand this we are more likely to receive His comfort—a supernatural comfort that only Jesus can give. This is one aspect that makes Christianity unique from all the other religions of the world. Jesus' suffering becomes a magnet that draws a reluctant skeptic and melts a resistant heart.

1. RECOGNIZE: MY PERSPECTIVE IS LIMITED

I tend to see things in black and white. My husband sees more through the lenses of gray. Sometimes this causes good old marital conflict and other times it gives us a broader perspective on a situation. However both of our perspectives are severely limited.

I love the beach—the steady roar of the ocean, the never-ending sand. It's also hard to beat a peanut butter and jelly sandwich on cheap white bread mixed with few grains of sand. Depending on the weather, the sea and the sand speak to me both of God's power and His tranquility. But it is the vastness of the beach that most overwhelms me.

Sitting on the beach makes me feel insignificant in a good way. I imagine myself one tiny grain of sand on an entire planet of beaches. There is so much more going on than I can ever imagine. God is so much bigger, so much more powerful than my little self. Life is not all about me. My perspective is limited.

Sometimes when I have a burning issue on my heart I can exhaust myself trying to find the solution or attempting to get God's answer to my issue. I pray and pray but only silence responds. Doesn't He hear? Doesn't He care? Why won't He answer? Perhaps His seeming silence is beckoning me to enlarge my perspective. Could there be more going on here than my one little grain of sand?

When our twin daughters were six weeks old, our

boys two and four, and our eldest daughter had just turned seven, we moved from Pennsylvania to the DC area (northern Virginia). The twins had colic and I had no friends, no family, and no help. My husband was in his first job as a senior pastor and was gone a lot. I was totally sleep deprived and it was all I could do to stagger through the day. I felt like a complete failure. I could not live up to my expectations as a wife, a mother, or a ministry partner. My self-image hit a new low. Again and again I cried out to the Lord to make me a better mother, a better wife, to fix me. But nothing seemed to happen. For almost two years I just gutted it out, overwhelmed with numbness and guilt.

One day I read Jeremiah 33:3: "Call to me and I will answer you and will tell you great and hidden things that you have not known." As I thought about this passage I realized that perhaps God had something new He wanted to teach me. Could I be so focused on His fixing me and my situation that I was missing out on something else? Did He have something more, something different, some "other" that He desired for me to learn? He did. Gently He revealed to me that I had a big problem with pride. Because of my heritage and my personality I had been pretty successful in life. But now I felt like a failure. I could not fix things. These kids were going to be around a long time. Unbeknownst to me, my pride had grown and God enabled me to see more clearly this sin. In revealing to me my sin of pride, God also showed me that my theology had become confused. I felt ashamed that I wasn't living up to the standards I had set for myself. Somehow I felt God didn't love me or approve of me unless I performed well. In confessing my sin of pride I realized in a fresh way that God didn't love me because I was a good mother or good wife or doing good things for Him. I wasn't—in any way. Instead He loved me just because I belonged to Him. Period. Dealing with my pride ushered me into a deeper understanding of His grace, a grace that brings freedom. This incident was a beginning. I will never be cured of the sin of pride. It continues to rear its ugly head over and over but now I am more sensitive to recognizing it, confessing it, and experiencing His forgiveness.

But there was something else I learned through this experience. I learned that often we limit God. It's so easy to see Him with limited vision, to expect that He wants to do this or that in our lives. But He may very well want to reveal to us something new—something other.

Based on Jeremiah 33:3, I call this "the principle of the other." When I feel stuck or feel that God has me on hold and I'm not getting any answers to whatever my issue of the moment is, I go to God and ask Him, "Is there some other thing you want to show me in this situation?" And I wait, spending time in His Word and listening to Him. He may reveal a sin I've been denying, a fresh realization about Him, another way of looking at something, or an unexpected blessing. His revelation always broadens my perspective. It reveals to me a little bit more of how very big He is.

Today there is a determined red cardinal outside my big window. He has spent this day banging with fury on the windowpane. Occasionally he takes a dive bomb and I'm afraid he is going to knock himself out. Other times he just sits on the ledge and pecks at the window. He may think he sees an enemy or potential mate in front of him but the reality is that he's seeing his own reflection. He is angry and frightened. His actions are futile. His perspective is limited. I, on the inside, wish there were some way I could tell this poor frustrated bird that there is nothing to fear. But apart from covering the window or learning bird talk I have no solution. Looking at him with pity I realize how like him I am. I cannot see clearly or interpret reality easily. I get caught up in my own little world, trying to peck away at my issues, failing to see what is true. But I have a heavenly Father who sees all. He understands my limitations. He feels my frustration and He offers me a greater perspective. He is up to something in my life and in yours. And it is good. In His everlasting arms, we can find peace, we can receive comfort, and we can experience a fresh vision of just how big He is.

"Call to me and I will answer you, and will tell you great and hidden things that you have not known" (Jeremiah 33:3).

A TIME TO REFLECT:

1. We have seen how important it is to be around folks unlike us. Our perspective on life and our perspective on God will grow when we step out of our own world. If you are a parent, how can you expose your kids to people unlike themselves? Plan one way to do this within the next month. If you do not have children at home, what is a way that you can be with someone unlike yourself within the next month? Ask another person to share their story with you.

2. As you read about some of the different times in Jesus' life, what did you find that was the most comforting to you? How does this insight enlarge your vision of God?

3. Have you recently felt or said to yourself, *No one really understands how hard this (your issue of the moment) is for me.* Name your current issue. Think about the life of Jesus and ask: where in His life did He experience what I am feeling? If you are unfamiliar with the life of Jesus, simply ask a friend who knows Him to help you do this. Both of you will be encouraged.

FOR FURTHER STUDY:

It's show time!
And you are the director and producer of this reality

show. So get ready for a fun and unique Bible study that just might give you a new perspective on a real story.

1. Read Luke 2:22-38.
2. Read it a second time and list the characters in this passage.
3. Now take one character at a time and write down everything you learn about this character from this passage. Don't rush through this.
4. Add to each character description the feelings they might have been experiencing. Use your imagination. How would you have felt if you were in their role? (Use a different color pen for this.) How do their perspectives differ?
5. Go back and re-read the passage and consider God's role in this segment. What do you learn about His character? Write down everything you notice. Some of His traits will be inferred or assumed. Don't miss these. (You might do this several times because different things will pop out during each reading.)
6. How do the things you notice in this scene about the character of God apply in your life? Use a new colored pen for this.
7. Spend some time thanking God for the particular insights He has given you.

CHAPTER EIGHT

REFOCUSING WHEN THINGS GET BLURRY

When I got glasses in second grade I was overwhelmed by what I could see and shocked by what I had assumed was reality but actually was not. Suddenly my entire world became clear. Things were so much better than I had imagined. However, as I approached the teen years, I became embarrassed by my very thick lenses. They were definitely not cool in those days. Contacts were just being developed and I was thrilled when my ophthalmologist prescribed a set for me. They took some getting used to but as I persisted, I came to love them. My vision was clear and I was not as embarrassed by my looks. Over the years medical technology has vastly improved contacts. But they still get dirty, they still get scratched, and I often get frustrated when cleaning them. It's so easy for pollen or dust, makeup or sweat and even tears to clog them up causing my vision to become cloudy. After I thoroughly wash them or sometimes replace them, I find the beauty of a clear focus return.

In my faith journey I have found that over and over again it is easy for me to let my issues, whatever the main concern of the moment is, get in the way of my view of God.

We all have issues. It doesn't matter if we are male or female, young or old, Asian, Caucasian, African, (etc.), married, single, divorced, or widowed. Having a burden (issue or concern) is simply a normal part of living in a fallen world and being human.

Our issues will change depending upon our season in life.

Over the years I have found it helpful to see life in terms of seasons. We have biological seasons: childhood, single years, marriage for some, parenting years (and within this season parenting toddlers and parenting teens is very different), empty nest, bungee cord season (a season when you thought you were an empty nester and your kids came home again), the golden years, and perhaps singleness again. We also have seasons of loss: a death, the loss of a dream, the loss of health. We have mixed up seasons, like caring for an elderly parent while raising a toddler. And we have seasons of transition, of change. We tend to think that stability is the norm, but in reality transition is the norm and stability is the rare exception. Recognizing and accepting this will give us a better perspective. Every season will have both challenges and blessings. It is important to articulate the challenges but then choose to focus on the blessings.

One of the challenges of the baby/toddler years is frustration. You don't feel like you accomplish anything. You get up in the morning, get the house picked up, the kids fed, and by evening it's all a mess again. Reflecting on your day you don't feel like you completed anything. It's particularly hard if you are used to a challenging job with a list of things you can check off as done at the end of each day. And in the market place you have affirmation and a salary. But at home?

So a challenge for you might be frustration. On the other hand, one of the blessings unique to this season is that toddlers say the funniest things. Caleb's mother planted a big wet kiss on his cheek at bedtime. "Oh," exclaimed Caleb, "Mommy, wipe off the wet but not the love!" Saying funny things is a blessing unique to this season of young children. Teenagers don't say very funny things. A challenge of the teen years is setting limits and letting go. When should we stand firm? However a blessing, particularly of the latter years, is that you begin to see the pay-off of some early years of parenting. Your teen might actually ask what she could do to help with dinner. Personally, I loved the teen years but different seasons will appeal to each of us. The principle is to articulate the challenges of your current season but then choose to focus on the blessings.

No matter what season of life we are in our issues can cloud our view of God. An issue will slowly distort my reality. Why is this? Our thoughts are more likely to be centered around our concern than focused on our God. In our heads we mull over our issues. Like a cow chewing his cud over and over again. We contemplate how to fix things, avoid things, or get through things.

My husband is a horseman. He loves to ride them, brush them, talk to them (because they don't talk back!), and watch races on TV. The Triple Crown is a big calendar event in our lives. No matter what we are doing, everything stops when these three races come on the television. We never cease to be thrilled and nervous as we watch these magnificent animals begin the parade to the track. One of the last things a jockey usually does before entering the starting gate is to adjust his goggles. Generally made of plastic, they are worn to prevent injury and to enable him to see while dirt and turf are kicked back during a race. This year's Kentucky Derby was particularly wet. Garry Stevens, who won three derbies as a jockey, commented, "You can see the jockeys wearing up to ten pairs of goggles. When you've got that many layers of goggles stacked up, everything becomes distorted. Your vision is impaired significantly."

Just as a jockey has to throw back his dirty goggles in order to be able to see clearly, I have to clean my contact lenses in order to be able to see without distortion. In a similar way I often have to cleanse my spiritual eyes in order to obtain a more accurate vision of God.

Too often in the moment, my mental eyes are clouded with concerns. I'm anxious about an interview, a decision that has to be made, a child or friend in crisis. Sometimes I simply feel anxious and can't even pinpoint the source of my anxiety. In the midst of jumbled emotions, I forget who God really is. I forget how very much He loves me and how He longs to protect and guide me and provide for me. Once again I long for a clearer picture of how big He really is.

Several actions will help us clarify our vision of God and in turn we will see our issues from His perspective rather than from our own very limited, myopic, narrow viewpoint.

ASK YOURSELF, "WHERE ARE MY EYES?"

When I ask myself this question I realize that my eyes (my thoughts) are usually in one of three places—either on myself, on others, or on my circumstances.

If my eyes are on myself I can quickly become disappointed in who I am or who I am not. *I'm not pretty. I'm not smart. I can't do this. I can't succeed in this job. I'm a failure.* Focusing on myself rapidly leads to self-condemnation—a pit so easy to fall into and so difficult to climb out of.

Often I realize that hidden in this pit is the sin of pride, masquerading as low self-esteem. Pride rears its ugly head when I think too much of myself *or* too little of myself. Genuine humility is God-focused not self-focused.

If my eyes are on others it is easy to fall into the comparison trap. *She seems to handle everything and I can't. Her life is perfect and mine is falling apart. She has lots of friends and I don't. He's successful and I never will be. Her husband is affectionate and mine is cold as ice.* When we look at others we have to remember there is always data missing. That gal who seems able to handle everything or whose life seems perfect may have a painful relationship with a colleague or a family member. That husband who is affectionate may have a difficult relationship with a child. That guy who is successful in the market place may have a marriage that is crumbling. There is always data missing. No one has it all together. It's a false perception. We are all broken.

If my eyes are on my situation it can be easy to succumb to a case of the "if onlys" as mentioned in chapter 2. "*If* only" I had an exciting career. "If only" I weren't from a dysfunctional family. "If only" I had a husband or a wife. "If only" I could get out of debt. "If only" I had a real friend. If we persist in mulling over the negatives of our situations we are merely fertilizing the weeds of self-pity. Hardy weeds which grow rapidly to choke out joy.

In each of these examples we recognize a common thread: self-focus. A focus that leads to self- pity or to pride.

So what do we do?

We cannot put blinders on like a trainer often puts on a racehorse to force him to keep his focus straight ahead thereby avoiding distraction by the other horses. No, we have to learn to look at ourselves, at others, and at our circumstances through the prism of God's character.

FOCUS ON WHO HE IS

A few years ago I realized that when I woke up and began to think about my day I became depressed. There was no prevailing reason why, simply a feeling of dread followed by guilt for feeling this way.

Mothers of young children don't have the luxury of thinking before they get out of bed. More likely there's some little foot kicking them or a big voice screaming for them. But some of us don't have kids. Others have reached the season when we do have a few minutes to awaken and the time to contemplate. It can be a moment of rejoicing or a moment of feeling blue. It depends upon our focus. Lying in bed that morning I realized I needed to adjust my attitude, to shift from thinking about how I feel about my day to focusing on God. Paul tells us in Romans 12:2: "Do not be conformed to this world but be transformed by the renewal of your mind that by testing you may discern what is the will of God what is good and acceptable and perfect." It was a different kind of wake-up call for me.

In the gospel of John there is a scene in which Jesus is talking with His disciples as He tries to prepare them for His death. He says, "But the Helper, the Holy Spirit, whom the Father will send in my name, he will teach you all things and bring to your remembrance all that I have said to you" (John 14:26).

To stop my habit of thinking negatively as I woke up I began to ask the Holy Spirit to *remind me* of one character trait of God the Father or of His Son that I could meditate on that day. I lay still until one became clear to me.

I remember the first day I did this the trait that I thought of was *He is a God who **rescues*** (Psalm 18:19, Psalm 91: 14-16). Hoping out of bed with more joy than usual I went to get a cup of tea when my phone rang. A friend on the line burst into tears, "Susan," she exclaimed, "I'm having so much trouble with my teenage son. I feel like he needs to be rescued." Can you imagine the joy that flooded my heart? It was as if the Holy Spirit placed an exclamation point over His leading.

On another day the character trait was *He is a God who **lavishes*** (Ephesians 1:8). As I thought about God lavishing His love on me I realized how radical that was. Too often I act as if He parcels out his love, trickle by trickle, drip by drip, definitely sparingly, without waste. Oh no! He lavishes. Contemplating this fact changed my entire day!

One morning I awoke paralyzed with indecision. There was a decision I had to make and I did not know what to do. I didn't trust my instincts. I needed Him to lead, to direct, to speak. But would He? I turned in my regular reading to Psalm 29, and saw repeatedly the phrase: *the voice of the Lord.* Yes. He would speak in His time in His way. Sometimes His timing seems slow. I am impatient. But I can have the assurance that He will **speak.**

For many years I have continued this habit. Sometimes I forget and then slowly the morning blues return. I realize I need to resume my habit. Psalm 90:14 states, "Satisfy us in the morning with your steadfast love that we may rejoice and be glad all our days." This small practice has changed my attitude and enabled me to focus more on Him throughout each day.

In Appendix 2 you will find a list of thirty-one traits, one for each day of the month. I share these with the hope that it will encourage you to begin this practice as well.

A second habit to help me focus more on Christ actually rose out of frustration with an often-quoted verse in Scripture. Paul exhorts us, "Do not be anxious about anything, but in everything by prayer and supplication with thanksgiving let your requests be made known to God. And the peace of God, which transcends all understanding, will guard your hearts and your minds in Christ Jesus" (Philippians 4:6-7).

"Susan," a friend said, "You don't have to be anxious, just give your worry to God and He'll give you His peace." Really? The harder I tried to do this the more I failed. I would empty my brain giving Him my worry and waiting for His peace which seem so illusive and then seconds later I'd be back to worrying again. I really came to dislike this Scripture! Yes, I have the worry gene. However, I knew that His Word is more powerful than my concern. I had to be missing something.

Then I read the following verses, "Finally brothers and sisters, whatever is true, whatever is honorable, whatever is just, whatever is pure, whatever is lovely, whatever is commendable; if there is any excellence, if there is anything worthy of praise, think about these things ..." (Philippians 4:8-9). I realized I could not merely empty my brain without replacing my anxious thoughts with something else. Lovely, true, noble, pure, etc. describe the character of God. So instead of merely giving my worries to God and waiting for His peace I began to say His character traits out loud, as many as I could think of. *You are the truth. You know everything. Nothing is hidden from You. In You there is light and there is no darkness at all. You are able.* Speaking out loud helps me to focus on Him rather than on my worries and in the process, peace comes. Of course worry creeps back in and I have to begin all over again. But in the process He becomes bigger than my concern.

I love to run. I don't use headphones, primarily because I like the quiet. Often when I run I use the time to go through the alphabet asking God to show me a character trait of His for each letter. Sometimes I do this when I have trouble sleeping or if my imagination is out of control—running to fear and I need to rein it in. Recently I reached "V" in my alphabet litany and I began to contemplate the fact that ours is a God who *visits*. It was a delightful time of recalling the stories of God's visiting folks, sometimes unexpectedly, throughout the Old Testament. He visited Moses in the burning bush (Exodus 3:2). He visited Elijah when he was curled up in a cave resting after a forty-day trip (1Kings 19: 8-9). He visited Abraham to tell him Sarah would have a son (Genesis 18:10). In the New Testament, I remembered his visit to the Virgin Mary to tell her she would give birth to Jesus (Luke 1:29-33). He visited Paul to warn him not to enter Bithynia and instead proceed to Troas (Acts 16:7-8). Remembering His visits in the stories of the Bible gave my faith a boost that He would visit me. He has my back covered. If you are not familiar with the Word of God it will be harder to do this but that's where friends come in. Ask friends to tell you of times in their lives when God has visited them. It will not likely be an angel as it was so often in the stories of the Bible (although it could be), but it will be a time when they had an unusual sense of His presence, His comfort, and His leading. When we recall the times God has led us in the past it builds our faith in order that we might trust Him in the present. Hearing stories from others enlarges our view of God.

BE ALERT TO TOO MUCH SPIRITUAL SELF-FOCUS

My young friend was in a hard place. He was newly married and had no job. A deeply committed believer, he was struggling with God. Many times he cried out to Him, "God, what are you doing in my life? Am I doing something wrong? Why aren't you leading me?" Thorough self-examination provided no answers. He was simply stuck.

A talented woman became president of a new company.

She had a seminary degree and a love of teaching. She knew virtually nothing about business. But now she found herself running a company. Totally out of her comfort zone she cried out to the Lord, "What are you doing? Why am I here? What purpose do you have in this? What am I suppose to learn?" There were no clear answers.

Sometimes we can work ourselves up into a frenzy trying to figure out what God is doing and why. And then we realize: It is really none of my business what God is up to. He is God and He does not have to explain Himself to me. My job is to be faithful in whatever place He has put me for this season.

We can fall into the trap of taking our spiritual temperature too often. Of asking, "How am I doing with the Lord?" Of worrying if I'm pleasing Him, if I'm making the right decision. Today there's a lot of emphasis on calling, on discovering and using our gifts. While this is good, we must be cautious that we don't become too self-focused in trying to figure it all out. If we get too introspective, we can lose our joy and our peace.

Oswald Chambers says, "The continual grubbing on the inside to see whether we are what we ought to be generates a self-centered, morbid type of Christianity, not the robust simple life of a child of God."[1]

When I am really honest I realize that I just want to be God—to fix myself and everyone around me. But that's not my job. It's His. Sometimes what God is up to isn't really any of my concern. Even what He is up to in my own life. I'm His problem not mine. Sometimes I just need to lighten up and let go. And wait. Too much self-analysis can lead to the sin of trying to play God in my own life, a gruesome self- focus. I pray, "Lord please deliver me and John and all of our children and grandchildren from a morbid self-focus."

Be alert to having your eyes looking at yourself through magnifying glasses rather than at the Lord.

I have to remember I'm where I am with His permission. If I'm seeking Him, confessing my sins, and spending time in His Word, He will reveal to me what He's up to in His time and in His way. Meanwhile He may be simply saying rest, wait, and be alert to the "other" that He may want to reveal.

Sometimes "the other" may come in the form of a new direction or an unexpected blessing.

OPEN YOUR EYES TO THE UNEXPECTED BLESSING

Our daughter Libby and her husband McLean came face to face with God's work in a dramatic intervention. Here are their words:

> The news we received from my doctor in December 2009 was discouraging. "Your ovaries appear to be that of a forty-five year-old." I was thrity. This news combined with the fact that my body has never been able to ovulate on its own, made us realize that the gift of another biological child would truly be a miracle. This began a season of pleading with God: waiting, trying (with the help of ovulation shots), heartache, and tears.
>
> The focus of our prayers was on a child but God

chose instead to refine our marriage. We began to ask deeper questions of each other, questions that are so easy to gloss over in the routines of life. We gained a fresh vision of how much more deeply the Lord wanted us to grow in knowing Him, knowing each other, and knowing ourselves. It was then that we began to pray and tentatively pursue an Ethiopian adoption. This fragile conviction to adopt resulted in God further revealing to us the strength and love we had in the community that prayerfully surrounded us. This was a process of learning to relinquish control of the vision of how we thought we would grow our future family.

Our lives were being enriched in unexpected ways throughout this waiting process. The unexpected expression of God's love was humbling as we were able to see beyond our limited desires. In April, however, we finally had a positive pregnancy test! Our joy became disbelief when at our first ultrasound we heard these words, "You have four."

We prayed for a baby and got a deeper marriage. We prayed about an Ethiopian adoption and got a stronger community. We continued to pray for one more biological baby and we are having quadruplets. We have been amazed at God's leading. We have learned to ask boldly and surrender completely, and we pray that we will continue to do so as this adventure continues.

On the day of the quads' birth, John and I, along with

Kem and Norma (McLean's mom and dad) and various siblings, gathered in the Labor and Delivery lobby of Baptist Hospital in Memphis. Other families were also waiting for news of their own. Because this was a planned c-section we did not have to wait long before McLean came out to announce Libby had four healthy babies. In the midst of tears and sighs of relief we burst into singing the Doxology, "Praise God from whom all blessings flow. Praise Him all creatures here below. Praise Him above ye heavenly hosts. Praise Father, Son, and Holy Ghost." In a crowded hospital we experienced an unexpected holy moment.

MAKE SPACE FOR HOLY MOMENTS

We can't always program or plan holy moments. But what we can do is make space in our lives for them to occur. Recently our daughter Susy commented that the data on her phone was using up all of her storage. She had to go through her apps and figure out which she could live without and remove them to free up more space. Sometimes I imagine my brain as a computer with too many files open at once or a smart phone with too many apps clogging up the system. With the complications of life it is hard to create a quiet space in which we might hear God speak to us in new ways. So distracted are we that it is hard to focus. Sometimes I long for complete quiet, not only a literal silence but a quiet in my head, an emptying of sorts, a setting aside of concerns in order that I might be more open to His voice. The discipline of listening prayer prescribed by *Lectio Devina* is one helpful way to quiet our heads and open our hearts to hearing from God. A discipline I have just begun is to take a few moments throughout each day and simply say, "Quiet my thoughts, oh Lord, and let me hear your voice." And I try to be still and simply listen.

Perhaps your eyesight, like mine, gets blurry. Glasses become scratched and prescriptions have to be updated. Contacts may need to be replaced. An infection might call for an antibiotic. Surgery may be needed to correct vision. Whatever the reason, when I can't focus properly it makes me feel disoriented and grouchy. And I don't like that feeling. I want to see with complete clarity. And like you, I long to see God as He really is.

Father we pray, enlarge our vision so we might see you more and more each day as you really are, our great big Father God. "Open my eyes that I might behold wondrous things out of your law [your word]"(Psalm 119:18).

A TIME TO REFLECT:

1. What is most likely to cloud your view of God? Is there an immediate issue that has grown bigger in your eyes than God?
2. Often our eyes are in one of three places: ourselves, others, or our circumstances. Of these three, which one do you identify with the most?
3. Is there a suggestion that you found helpful in this chapter that you plan to implement this week? What is it and why did you choose it?
4. List three to five character traits of God that you want to focus on this week.

FOR FURTHER STUDY:

1. What disciplines do you need to adopt (or things to lay aside) in order to gain a clearer vision of who God is?
2. Read Psalm 103 and Psalm 145 and make a list of every character trait of God you see in these selections.
3. Remembering the promise in John 14:26, ask God to reveal to you one character trait each day to focus on. (See Appendix 2 for an example.)
4. Write your own Psalm to the Lord with a particular emphasis on His character traits for which you are thankful.

CHAPTER NINE

WHY IS IT SO HARD TO BE THANKFUL?

My husband and I were staying in a rural village in Muranga, Kenya. The roads to Muranga were dangerous, unpaved, dusty, and filled with potholes. We drove by shacks that were taped together, children playing in the dirt, men sitting on cans swatting flies. Our hosts were Bishop Julius and Nellie Gachuche. They had invited us to speak to pastors in this remote area. African women clothed in vivid colors had walked many miles bringing food to welcome us. Our living quarters were simple yet Nellie gave us the best beds with mosquito netting. I'm not sure where she slept or even if she did. When I awoke the first morning she was already up with a breakfast banquet prepared in our honor. As I walked into the room a beaming Nellie greeted me,

"Susan," She exclaimed, "a miracle has occurred!"

"What?" I responded expecting some huge event.

"Why, I woke up." She replied, smiling from ear to ear.

Stunned, I could barely respond.

Nellie's attitude shamed me. From the world's perspective she had so little. But in true reality she had so much—a spirit that noticed the ordinary and called it a miracle! She had a truly grateful heart. Oh how I long to be like Nellie.

Why Is It So Hard to Be Grateful?

Of all the things we have to do in life thanking God should be one of the easiest. Yet day in and day out it is one of the hardest things to do. Why is this? Several reasons come to my mind and I am sure you will have others.

We're too busy. Too often I find myself thinking, *I'll take time to praise God when life calms down.* The reality is life will never calm down. It only gets more complicated, more intense. We can become addicted to busyness. It gives an adrenalin rush until we crash.

We don't feel like it. I'm just not in the mood. Things are too hard right now. We assume we'll wait until we *feel* like it. Rarely will that happen and often it is when things are hard that we most need to praise God.

My friend Carmita was three months pregnant when she realized she was having a miscarriage. This was to be their third child so she recognized what was happening and ran into the bathroom while calling her husband Reuben. It was after midnight. She did indeed lose the baby and as they gazed sobbing at the tiny baby, Reuben said something shocking, "Carmita love, I really feel that we should thank God right now." Although she was crying, Carmita agreed. They both remember saying something like, "Lord this is really hard, but we choose to thank you. You are good. We praise you. Our lives are in your hands." An overwhelming sense of peace filled their hearts and they were bonded together in marriage in a deeper way than ever before. But this wasn't all. The next morning a friend, who had not heard about their loss, called Carmita. After she explained what had happened, their friend inquired with hesitation, "I have a very strange question. At any time last night did you thank the Lord? I ask because in the middle of the night the Lord woke me up with a clear message for you that filled me with joy: 'Tell Carmita and Reuben I accept their sacrifice of praise. I am pleased with them. '" This became a marker moment in their lives. God honored their obedience to praise Him, even in the midst of their grief. Thirteen years later Carmita says she still weeps when she recalls this time, "I felt so very, very loved by the Lord. "

Carmita and Reuben definitely did not feel like praising God. But they did it anyway and experienced the mysterious blessings of the sacrifice of praise and thanksgiving. They were overwhelmed by their heavenly Father's peace and love.

Thanking God in the midst of a tragedy is pure discipline. It does not mean we feel good nor does it make everything all right. Life hurts. As we've seen in chapter seven, Jesus identifies with our pain. He cries with us. Indeed our tears are so precious to God that the Psalmist says, "You have kept count of my tossings, put my tears in your bottle. Are they not in your book?"(Psalm 56:8). Some say that this is a picture of God collecting all the tears we shed on the earth and holding them gently for us in a bottle. (1)

We're lulled into taking things for granted. Including God's goodness. Especially those of us living in luxury of the west. Most of us do not struggle for food or clothes, nor do we worry about health (at least the young don't!). We just expect it or assume we will be able to do what we want, when we want. My mother used to say, "Be careful not to fall into the sin of presumption." Too often I know I presume upon God. I take His blessings for granted. As parents we get frustrated when our children do not appreciate things. They just want more. In my relationship with God I am so like my child. I expect but then fail to appreciate. Nellie's "miracle" made me realize how much I take God's goodness for granted.

The enemy does not want us to praise God. One of Satan's tricks is to keep us from praising and thanking God. Why? Because thanking God is pure worship. And in worship the power of the Holy Spirit is unleashed. When we chose to praise God something powerful takes place. His supernatural comfort and peace are poured out within our hearts, even the most broken. The Scriptures say "the praise of children silences the enemy" (Psalm 8:2). We long for the evil one's whispers into our heads to be silenced. When we praise Him, the enemy's power is broken. Praise is both countercultural and counterintuitive in our me-centered age.

When we begin to praise Him our perspective changes. The old hymn says it well, "Turn your eyes upon Jesus, look full in His glorious face and the things of this world will grow strangely dim in the power of his glory and grace." It doesn't say "things" will disappear but that they will dim. Music is a tool for praise. I cannot carry a tune but when I sing praises out loud to God my faith gets an infusion. When we praise God His supernatural power is unleashed. When we view our issues from His perspective, our issue, whatever it is at the moment, becomes smaller as we focus on His almighty power.

"I've tried to be grateful and I never seem to get anywhere."

One day I was in my laundry room trying to catch up on endless piles of dirty clothes. My laundry room was a mess. And at that moment it reflected the condition of my heart. Simply put I was feeling down, discouraged, overwhelmed with exhaustion, bored, and lonely. I wasn't the wife I should be, and I felt like a failure as a parent. The clutter around me only intensified my feelings of failure. Instead of being thankful I was engaged in a self-pity party. Self-condemnation reared its ugly head. *Susan you should be thankful but you can't even do that.* Although I knew the importance of a thankful heart and had tried to practice thankfulness it didn't seem to last. I was even weary of trying. At that moment I noticed a tired old poster stuck on the wall by the washing machine. It read, "... You have made me glad ..." (from Psalm 21:6). This was a pivotal moment for me. In reading the words of the faded old poster, I saw for the first time that I couldn't even make myself glad. I had to rely on Him to do even that. My spiritual poverty was far greater than I had imagined. How humbling this was and yet how freeing. Now when I don't feel like being thankful I ask, "Father I can't even thank you without your help. Please make me glad in you." When I begin in a step of faith to praise Him, in time He brings my feelings to a place of His supernatural peace.

This small moment in my laundry room became a large step in my faith journey—another way of looking at the juxtaposition of natural growth (becoming independent) and spiritual growth (becoming dependent). For me it was a further step in the humbling of a believer. I had to depend on His power—even to thank Him!

It is curious to me that in the Scriptures the word sacrifice is often used with the words praise, thanksgiving, and offering. Why?

"The one who offers thanksgiving as his sacrifice glorifies me; to one who orders his way rightly I will show the salvation of God!" (Psalm 50:23). "Through him then let us continually offer up a sacrifice of praise to God that is, the fruit of lips that acknowledge his name" (Hebrews 13:15).

Perhaps God knows us so well that He understands that many times for us to praise Him involves a sacrifice. I'm sure that is the way Carmita felt when in the midst of her miscarriage she and her husband chose to praise God simply for who He is. Praising God isn't always easy. It certainly involves sacrifice in a tragic situation. Yet even in the mundane, we set aside something else merely to praise Him. And what a tender loving Father He is to recognize our tiny sacrifices.

In struggling to be more proactive in thanking God I have found that thanksgiving has a twin—trust.

TWINS: TRUST AND THANKSGIVING

Our twin daughters Susy and Libby have always been

close. Although they are fraternal they look very much alike. For most of their lives they shared a small nine-foot by ten-foot bedroom. When big sister Allison went to college, Susy took over her room. But many nights I heard a slight noise in the hall as Libby tiptoed to sleep in her twin's room. They simply found comfort in being together. Of course they had the normal sibling fights growing up, but on the whole, they stood together against the world and often against us, their parents! They were and still are a team. Their personalities are different but they seem to complement each other. And when they are together they operate as a unit. Twins often have something very special the rest of us can't quite understand.

In a similar way, trust and thanksgiving act as twins. They feed each other. They complement each other. When we understand this partnership we become the beneficiary. Both our trust in God and our gratitude towards Him will grow.

So often I struggle to trust. The more I try to trust God the more frustrated I can become. Frustration gives way to introspection and once more to self-condemnation. *Why can't I trust you in this situation, God? I should be able to.* I am beginning to discover that if I focus on who God is—His character traits—and take time to thank and praise Him for them, my ability to trust grows. Too often our mentality is to try to work up trust and then if He comes through I'll thank Him. But it is much easier to trust if we spend time thanking Him first. A healthy diet, regular exercise, and enough sleep enable us to have the energy to function well and grow properly. In a similar way, the practice of thanksgiving enables us to grow in trusting God more completely. In thanking Him we allow the magnitude of His goodness to over whelm us.

Author Sarah Young says, "Trust and thankfulness will get you safely through this day. Trust protects you from worrying and obsessing. Thankfulness keeps you from criticizing and complaining; those 'sister sins' that so easily entangle you." (2)

I readily identify with the father whose son was possessed by an impure spirit. When he brought the boy to Jesus he asked Him to have pity on him and help him, if He could. Jesus was quick to reply, "If you can! All things are possible for one who believes." Immediately the father of the child exclaimed, "I believe; help my unbelief" (Mark 9:23-24). Like this father I too want to believe, to trust Him more. What a relief to know He will enable me to trust Him more and more. When I take time to thank Him I am making deposits into a trust account. It is piling up. Thanksgiving and trust are twins that will enable growth as God does His work in us.

HOW CAN I CULTIVATE A DISCIPLINE OF THANKSGIVING?

I can't, on my own. I need Him to make me glad, to do it within me. And so over and over again I ask Him to make me thankful. It's humbling, but David reminds us of God's promise, "He leads the humble in what is right and teaches the humble his way" (Psalm 25:9).

A wise person once said: "Sow a thought, reap an action; sow an action, reap a habit; sow a habit, reap a character, sow a character, reap a destiny." Small habits of thanksgiving can reap a huge destiny—a legacy of thanksgiving and trust. Here are several to inspire you to develop your own.

Utilize special prayers

For a number of years I have met regularly with six young ministry wives. They come to my home for dinner approximately every other Monday night. We laugh, cry, share deeply, and pray together. We have come to know each other very well and our bonds are tight. I love these girls. For a season we decided to begin our time by praying together using the ACTS formula (adoration, confession, thanksgiving, supplication). Often when we gather we are harried and stressed and we simply need time to refocus and calm down. As each girl arrives she tiptoes into the family room where we curl up on the soft, blue rug and simply praise God for who He is. This is adoration. Adoring God for who He is, praising Him for His character traits. *Thank you Lord that you are still in charge. You are not caught off guard by anything that happens. You are full of mercy. You formed me in my mother's womb and you know me better than I know myself. You are delighting in me at this very moment. Your kindness does not fail. You are full of mercy.* And we have times of silence. Usually when we pray with friends we pray about concerns (supplication). Sometimes we remember to thank Him. However, we are most unlikely to take time to purely adore Him. We have found this little formula helpful in reminding us to praise (adore) Him for who He is, to confess our sins to one another and Him, to thank Him for the specific things He has done for us, and then to offer our requests (supplications) to Him. Doing this together gives us a window into one another's lives. And by the time we get up to eat dinner we feel refreshed in our spirits. Praising God restores our perspective.

Set up altars of thanksgiving.

Throughout the Old Testament we see many examples of God doing amazing things for the children of Israel. Usually the Israelites were quick to recognize His mighty hand and to honor Him. To help them remember His work they built altars or monuments. In the future, when they became discouraged or doubted His involvement in their lives, the monuments would serve to remind them of what He had done and therefore to spur them to believe He would come through for them again. And they would tell their children what God had done.

When our five children were small, a huge tornado-like storm swept through our back yard, ripping a giant tree from its roots and throwing it through the kitchen ceiling into the area where moments before I had been feeding four small children. Cabinets crashed off the walls, china plates exploded into sharp projectiles covering the area. I had just left the kitchen and was bathing children in another area of the house. It was truly a miracle we were not sitting at the table and killed.

Once the cleanup was completed I placed a large rock at the spot where the tree had been. I wanted the rock to remind me over the years of this time that God protected us. And I want to show my grandchildren the rock and tell them the story of God's protection.

Establish simple traditions.

When Allison was about eighteen months old we visited the old family farm in North Carolina. There's a hammock in the front yard that overlooks the fields. Each day we would climb together into the hammock for a swing and while we swung we sang our "Thank You God" song. I began by thanking God for something and then it was her turn. We took turns back and forth. "Thank you God for trees. Thank you God for my dog," and so forth. It was not a big deal. It was a simple tradition—an offering to our heavenly Father and a reminder of His blessings to us. Even today when I swing in our own hammock I recall our thank you song and it inspires me to take a moment to thank Him all by myself.

My friend Judy has designated elevators as a place of praise. When she takes the elevator to the intensive care unit of the hospital where she volunteers to hold babies, she praises God. She praises Him for His love for the smallest infant, for His tenderness, for His healing power.

Linda, a college professor, has chosen the gym parking lot as a chapel of thanksgiving. As she walks in to workout she takes time to intentionally thank God that she is able to walk, talk, smile, and exercise. She thanks Him that she has the time and money to join a gym and she prays for those she will encounter. Whenever she can, she parks in the same spot because this helps to remind her that her spot is holy ground—a place of thanksgiving

Pause and praise.

It's good to create special monuments where we take time to praise Him but it's also helpful to learn to be spontaneous. Too often we fail to thank Him because we think we have to make it a big deal. Hence we never get around to it. It doesn't have to be a big deal at all. God delights in the tiniest step.

I love cows. When I go for a run in the country I pass by a farm with cows. Today as I passed a mama cow with a baby I called out, "Hey cow. You are a good mama. Thank you Lord for cows!" Silly? Perhaps. But I do think God is delighted that I like His cows. I imagine it brings Him joy when I tell him so—just like it does when my child spontaneously tells me he likes something I made for him. I find it helpful to thank God out loud. It keeps my mind from wandering.

Ann Voskamp wrote a book about the practice of thanksgiving. *One Thousand Gifts* quickly became a best-seller. Why? I believe the tremendous response to this book reveals that we have an inherent need, often unrecognized, to praise our heavenly Father and something deep within us knows this is so. We can relate to her story as she struggles to establish a discipline of thanksgiving.

Worship regularly in a church.

The writer of the book of Hebrews warns us—do not forsake meeting together but instead encourage one another (Hebrews 10:25). Part of a healthy spiritual diet is the weekly commitment to worship with a body of believers. Author Dr. Dan Allender has an interesting insight about worship. He says that one of the important reasons for us to worship while we are on this earth is that it will prepare us for worship in heaven. We will not be prepared for what incredible worship we will experience in heaven if we have not learned to worship on earth.[3]

Our place of worship should have good biblical teaching as well as rich worship. Worship is not performance but instead a vehicle which enables us to turn our eyes and hearts toward Him in praise and thanksgiving. Music plays a significant role in our worship and there's not one right style. Variety is needed and your best friend may prefer a style completely different from yours. That's fine. The role of music is to lift us into His presence and enable us to worship Him in spirit and truth. Yes we can worship Him in privacy but we also need to be with others in worship, particularly when we are feeling down.

Recall frequently.

When we read the Old Testament we will notice how many times the children of Israel got discouraged and their faith (trust) in God began to weaken. When this occurred, both Moses and later Joshua would take time to remind the Israelites of what God had done for them in the past (Deuteronomy 32). This bolstered their faith and enabled them to believe He would be faithful in the present and future trials. The key word here is *remember*. Several years ago in a denominational split we lost all of our church property, its money, and our house. Naturally we were disappointed and wondered what the future would bring. The next day while I was spending some time alone with the Lord I wrote down all the ways He had specifically shown His faithfulness in our lives over many years. (One of the blessings of growing older is that you have *many* years!) I was amazed as I filled page after page of specific ways God had been good to us. This time of recalling and thanking Him bolstered my faith that He would indeed be faithful in the future.

Take time at the dinner table to recall with your children the specific ways each of you has seen God's goodness in the past week, the past year. Do the same thing with friends over a meal. The joy of hearing how God has been faithful in the lives of others will put deposits in your trust account to encourage you to believe He will handle your current issue and your future challenges.

In our desire to practice the discipline of thanksgiving we will have ups and downs. It may feel like a roller coaster. We may be on the rise for a while, rejoicing and thanking Him but then we plummet and discouragement, guilt, and shame take over. However just around the bend is another rise. The point is not to stay at the top of the roller coaster. The fun is in enjoying the whole ride. God understands our dips. Remember He knows we are but dust (Psalm 103:14). God isn't interested in perfection. He rejoices in the tiniest steps of progress. He knows we are weak. Nurturing a heart of gratitude is a lifelong process characterized by more failings than successes, but remember—God is generous. He cheers every time a word of praise or adoration enters our heads and leaves our lips. Simply ask Him to make you glad, again and again. He will. All we have to do is to call on Him and say, "God I'm in the dumps, I don't feel like praising you but I need to. Make me glad. Give me words of praise to utter." And then open your mouth.

My husband had another special moment with Nellie. She and her husband, Bishop Julius, took John for a long day to minister to some of the rural Kenyans. Their old car was rusty, bent up, covered with holes, and had four unreliable tires. Under most circumstances it was not fit for use. The road they traveled was unsafe and a car jacking was an ever-present danger. One had to avoid leaving a car parked for fear of tires or parts being stolen from it. Before they left for the trip they spent time praying for their day. Exhausted and filthy from strains of heat and the conversations of the day, they finally returned home at dusk. John quickly began to open the door when Nellie gently laid her hand on his arm.

"John, before we open the door we must thank Him for all of the provisions of this day. He has been so good to us."

My tendency is to pray a lot before an event. But how easy it is for me to forget to pray after the event, to thank Him and to marvel at the many examples of His provision.

I think I need to go live with Nellie.

"Great is the Lord and greatly to be praised, and his greatness is unsearchable. One generation shall commend your works to another and shall declare your mighty acts. On the glorious splendor of your majesty, and on your wondrous works, I will meditate" (Psalm 145:3-5).

A TIME TO REFLECT:

1. Do you find it hard to praise and thank God? Why do you think this is so? Recall a time when you did praise and thank Him. What was the result?
2. Do you know someone who is a person of praise and thanksgiving? How does spending time with her (or him) impact you?
3. What new habit will you begin this week that will enable you to grow in praise and thanksgiving?

FOR FURTHER STUDY:

1. Read Joshua 24. At the age of one hundred and ten, this is Joshua's farewell message to the children of Israel. What was the theme of his message? What things does he recall? What plea does he have for his followers? What are some of your take-aways from this chapter?
2. Think back over your life in ten-year segments. Write down the specific ways in which you see how God was faithful in certain situations during that decade, even if you did not realize it at that moment. It may help to pull out an old journal or photo album to recall memories. You might want to do this at several separate sittings, particularly if you are older! Don't rush through this but enjoy the process as a special time with your heavenly Father.

3. Ask Him now to make you glad. Open your mouth and praise Him for His specific character traits. It is helpful to do this out loud. Don't hurry. Ask Him to put in your head things for which He would love to be praised.

Section 3 Overview

A newborn baby's eyes are physically capable of seeing, but his brain is not yet ready to process all the visual information necessary to see clearly so his vision is fuzzy at birth. He doesn't know how to use his eyes in tandem so they may wander randomly. In the beginning he can't focus more than eight to twelve inches away—just far enough to make out your face! His eyes can detect light, shapes, and movement beyond, but it is pretty blurry. During the first couple of months of life he will learn to focus his eyes and track a moving object. We will see his progress if we hold our head close and move our eyes and watch as his little eyes begin to follow ours! Even though our child can see color at birth, his ability to distinguish tones is not yet developed. By four months he begins to develop depth perception and now his brain sends messages to his hand to reach out and grasp an object. At five months he is getting better at noticing small objects and tracking moving objects. And by eight months his vision is almost adult in clarity and depth perception. His attention will still be most focused on things close to him but he'll be able to recognize people across a room. (1)

Working together, his little brain and his eyes have developed remarkably. From birth, a child has all the equipment needed to focus clearly. However it takes time for all the parts to mature and to learn to work together. Each small step of growth opens up a larger world to our children.

Our vision of God is similar in many ways to the vision of a newborn. It is not yet fully developed. Like a new baby, our view of God is blurry. We have trouble focusing on Him. We can't clearly see all the ways He is at work. And we don't understand Him.

He is simply too big to grasp. Our faith is wobbly and we lack a clear picture of what He's up to.

A baby's sight develops in small increments. So does our faith. However, unlike an infant's eyes that are fully developed at about nine months, our view of God will not be fully developed this side of heaven. Only in heaven will we see Him in all His glory.

For now we remain spiritual infants. But that's all right! God is still at work. And we are growing in tiny increments in seeing how big He is. The rest of our lives we will be growing. Like a newborn baby we will gradually learn to see more clearly. Ours is a life full of new beginnings.

"Open my eyes Lord, I want to see Jesus ..."

CHAPTER TEN

BEGINNINGS

One would think the last chapter of a book would be entitled the summary or conclusion, something that leaves the reader with encouragement—now you know what to do, you can do it, and do it right. Something that enables you to feel accomplished!

But that's not really true in this case is it?

Although I've been mulling over the question, "Is God big enough?" for about fourteen years, I have only just begun to get a glimpse of how big He is. I am like a newborn whose eyes are barely open, only beginning to see clearly the glorious things that surround her. When I consider how big God is I am immediately struck with how little I really know Him.

Getting a bigger picture of God is a lifetime journey, not a new step in spiritual growth that we take and then move on to something else. For the rest of our lives we will be discovering how big our God really is. When we see Him face to face we'll realize all we learned in our time on earth was just a small glimpse compared to how big He really is in all His glory.

A HELPFUL DISTINCTION

As we gain a bigger view of God it helps to recognize another distinction between natural growth and spiritual growth. Both natural growth and spiritual growth are necessary but each has a very different role. It is a bit like putting in my contacts. My eyes are different so a unique lens is necessary for each eye in order that they might work together to enable me to see clearly.

Progress and product are necessary lenses for natural growth while *process and presence* are essential lenses for spiritual growth. It's another type of juxtaposition.

Progress is necessary for living in God's world. Where would we be without the progress made in medicine, in aviation, in engineering, in science, in technology? New products have been discovered and created that greatly benefit each of us. Developing these products has been painstaking, taking many years, long hours of research, and discipline. Most often, results have come one small step at a time.

In our personal lives, progress plays a significant role. We want to make progress in our careers, in our exercise classes, in our relationships, in our personal disciplines. We strive to attain that daily or long term goal. We teach our children self-discipline in order that they might make progress in school, on the field, in the band. Our job is to equip them in order that they might grow into healthy adults who will make a positive contribution to society.

Little steps of progress encourage us. Lack of progress is discouraging! One of the most discouraging things about being a young mother is that you don't see progress very often in raising kids. They still haven't learned to pick up their stuff, to say "thank you" and "please," or share toys with a sibling.

It's a false assumption to expect that satisfactory progress will always lead to a successful outcome—consistent training in a sport to a trophy, diligent work to a promotion, exercise and nutrition to health, wise parenting to a child who turns out right. When progress doesn't result in the goal we hoped for, we can feel like failures. As much as we'd like to, you and I cannot control the outcome. We may not get the promotion. Instead we could be fired. We may have taken care of our bodies and still get a terminal diagnosis. Our child may reject us and chose a lifestyle we believe is wrong.

Yes, progress and a satisfactory product can be very good things. But there is a hidden danger: It's easy to fall into the trap of using progress and product to determine our self worth.

Is my identity in accomplishments and success? If so, what happens when I fail? We will all fail.

My identity must rest in the fact that Jesus loves and accepts me, period. I am of great value simply because I am His. While progress and product can be good things, they must not determine our identity. Take care not to allow the wrong things to determine your sense of self-worth.

Similarly, while *progress* and *product* are necessary for natural growth, spiritual growth is more about *process* and *presence.* I believe God is ultimately more concerned about what we learn in the *process* of life than He is about our *progress.*

Let me tell you a story that I hope will illustrate this

concept.

We were away for a week of study leave. I was excited and hopeful about writing this final chapter. John was planning the fall sermon series. So it was to be a week of rest and productivity for both of us. Dear friends had loaned us their cabin in a beautiful mountain resort. Hydrangeas, impatiens, black eyed Susans, wild daisies, and carefully kept lawns seemed to blast out the glory of God. Trails weaving through woods and fields offered an unfolding pathway through His glorious creation. Friends were praying for our time away. It should have been a wonderful time of writing. But it wasn't. For the first five days I was stuck. No matter how long I sat at the computer, how much I prayed and read, nothing came. The few miserable sentences I wrote were just that, miserable. And to top it off, my foot hurt so I couldn't enjoy my usual runs. I felt really discouraged and down on myself. I wasn't producing anything. Those praying for the book were going to be disappointed. When the week was almost over I decided to look up verses having to do with joy since I had none.

I found myself in Habakkuk 3:17-19:

> Though the fig tree should not blossom, nor the fruit be on the vines, the produce of the olive fail and the fields yield no food, the flock be cut off from the fold and there be no herd in the stalls, yet I will rejoice in the Lord; I will take joy in the God of my salvation. God, the Lord, is my strength; he makes my feet like the deer's; he makes me tread on my high places.

Several things began to come together.

I recognized my self-worth had become dependent once again on progress and product. I was miserable because I wasn't producing. Progress and product are good qualities of natural growth and when we don't feel like we are making progress or producing a product it is normal to be frustrated or sad. That's ok. But there comes a point when those feelings become king over my emotions and they begin to control my disposition. When this happens, I need to ask: *Have I allowed progress and product to become idols?* In this case the answer was definitely yes. I also noticed Satan was multiplying my discouragement. This is one of his favorite tools.

The themes of progress and product had overruled the more important spiritual perspective of process and presence in my life. The humorous thing was that in writing about the difference between progress and process I myself fell into the trap of letting progress determine my self-worth. On the one hand I wasn't making any progress. But God had something "other" to teach me through this process (see chapter 7 for a description of the "other"). I had to learn again that process is far more important to God than what we produce. And I was not living in that truth. Instead I was losing hope because I wasn't seeing any progress. God is patient. He is not in a hurry. He has no deadlines. He is more concerned with molding us and shaping us into the people He has created us to be than He is with our accomplishments. His joy is in the process but mine wasn't. I just wanted to get there—to complete something.

There was another aspect to this. I knew I should

simply rejoice in the Lord. (Habakkuk 3:18) and I tried to but it wasn't very sincere because my lack of progress was getting in the way of seeing the Lord. It's hard to churn up joy. Once again Habakkuk spoke to me in verse 19, "He makes [enables] me ..."

He is the one who *enables* me. I have to ask Him to make me glad. I can't do it myself. I am completely dependent on Him. What I can do is choose to focus on who He is and how much His love for me is not dependent on my accomplishments. My self-worth is defined simply by the fact that I belong to Him. I am His precious child and so are you. Period.

God has such a sense of humor. I was convicted by my own words in a way that is funny. In this, God revealed to me yet again the reality of His interest in process. I needed His gentle reminder that what He is doing in my life in process is so much more important than producing a final product, a book. And I have to remember to rest in the assurance of His loving presence no matter what else is happening or not happening. At this very moment He is loving you and me not because of any accomplishment but simply because we are His.

It is tremendously helpful to distinguish between these themes of *progress* and *product* (natural growth) in contrast to the themes of *process* and *presence* (spiritual growth). All four are important in our lives but our tendency is most likely to focus on natural growth rather than spiritual growth. We must take care that we do not let progress and product become idols. And we must be attentive to what He might be teaching us in the process. His lessons in the process of our growth are often surprising and always transforming. These process lessons will give us a deeper glimpse into the character of our heavenly Father.

What about His Presence?

Our heavenly Father's heart is a heart of presence. He is present with you and me 24/7, even when we don't feel it or acknowledge it. He longs for us to be aware of Him and to enjoy His presence during the process of growing. On the wall opposite our bed I have painted a verse: "In His presence is fullness of joy" (from Psalm 16:11). This is to remind me in the morning that how I feel about my day is not nearly as important as experiencing His presence.

But what does His presence look like? How do we enter into it? Three visuals will help bring clarity to this opaque principal.

1. Stop gritting your teeth.

So much of my relationship with God is one of spiritual teeth gritting. I grit my teeth and work harder and harder to trust Him and then when I don't, I feel guilty. This brings to mind another juxtaposition of natural growth and spiritual growth that I just encountered. My friend Ann is dying. For seven years she has battled cancer like a warrior.

"Ann," I exclaimed, "you are my hero. You keep fighting. I don't know how you do it."

"Susan," she responded, "I am not a fighter, I am a surrender-er. I realize again and again that my life is about surrendering to God—my dreams, my sins, my hopes, and my will. And He replaces them with an unusual sense of His presence."

In natural life we do fight, we do endure, and we teach our kids to keep on, to persevere. As Winston Churchill said, "Never, never, never give up." However, spiritual life is about continual surrender. Daily, I must surrender my will to His. When I'm with Ann I feel like I am standing on holy ground. The peace of her surrender is overflowing with contentment and yes, even joy.

The answer to spiritual growth does not lie in trying harder to trust but in relaxing and simply getting to know the One in whom I want to place my trust. The more I know Him, the better I will be able to trust Him. The more I see how very big He is the more I will relax in His presence. The more I believe His perfect love and acceptance of me, the more I will stop striving and rest in Him.

2. Raise your umbrella and notice the sky.

In thinking about God's presence it helps me to visualize a giant umbrella above my head. Held by my hand it moves in concert with my movements. It does not leave me uncovered. It provides a steady shelter from whatever the weather might be. My umbrella enables me to notice and enjoy my surroundings or to continue a conversation while walking with a friend. Its presence enables me to keep on going, even in rough weather. In a similar way, no matter what the conditions are around me, I am covered by God's presence. Sometimes I say out loud to myself, "Right at this moment, I am covered and surrounded by the presence of my loving Father God."

Another image is that of the sky. God has given His sky

as a canopy over us. Genesis 1:1 tells us, "In the beginning God created the heavens and the earth." It was one of the first things He created. Night and day, season to season, His heavens are stationary. They are immovable. No matter what is going on under His skies it is always light way above. I doubt any of us have spent time worrying that we'll wake up one morning to find that the heavens have disappeared and nothing is there. His heaven just is. I like to imagine it as a symbol of His love. It's a canopy of His love over us. In the 70s, a song in Christian youth circles had the refrain "His banner over me is love."(1) Today it sounds a bit cheesy but the message is true and once again I've found myself singing the silly refrain. It has a way of reminding and reassuring me that He is in charge, He is immovable and His love for me is perfect.

3. Consider a ladder and a garden.

It helps me to recognize that our tendency is to live life as if it were a long ladder disappearing into the clouds with no end in sight. I visualize myself climbing to the next rung on the ladder—the next season in life, the next project, the next accomplishment. My attitude becomes, *When I just get to ___ then ___*. The next thing might be a good relationship, financial stability, the kids in school, the teens out of the house, a new career. But the reality is that every time I get to the next rung, the next thing, I look up and there's something else to get to. It never ends. I wonder if God would rather see us approach life as a garden rather than as a ladder?

Imagine all of the beautiful gardens of the world gathered in your state. The diversity of the plants and the array of colors would be overwhelming. You would not race through this garden. You would want to walk slowly down each path, careful not to miss anything. Along the way you'd notice rough spots. They might even appear bleak. But the bleakness would only serve to set off the surrounding beauty. You would not want this journey to end. The process of walking through this garden would be like tasting the delicacies of a delicious banquet prepared by the world's most famous chefs. Even more than the beauty of the process of looking at the flowers would be the presence of the master gardener.

I find it helpful to view His presence through the metaphor of a garden.

As I stand at the entrance to a beautiful garden my emotions collide. On one hand I'm excited and I can't wait to enter to see the beauty that has been created. But ever so often I'm fearful of disappointment. Will it be all that I have hoped for? The only way to find out is to take the first step into the garden.

In a similar way, stepping into a greater awareness of God's presence is enticing but also a little bit frightening. Will I be disappointed? Life is full of disappointments of things that happen and things that do not. It's part of living in this fallen world. However, God will not disappoint us. We may not understand His ways but we can rest in the assurance that He is good.

HOW DOES HE SEE US?

Throughout this book we've been discussing how we

see God. But how does He see us? He sees us with perfect vision, perfect understanding, and exhilarating hope. Too often our instinctive response to such a God is, *but God if you only knew, then ...* We forget He does know! He knows every thought, every sin, every fear, every failing. He is not shocked by us. He knows and His knowing is wrapped in compassion. It is for this very reason that Jesus died. He died that we might live. This is the ultimate juxtaposition.

Who sees more clearly? Whose eyes are more important? How I see myself is not nearly as important as how God sees me. My vision is severely limited.

God looks at you and me with perfect eyes and He sees a child of His own creation, a forgiven child, a child with a divine purpose. He longs for us to be completely assured of His love, a love that He will never withdraw.

But there's so much more

God has so much more for us than we can imagine. We see only in three dimensions. He has unlimited dimensions! Just contemplate what's under the ground, beneath the sea, what's hidden in the heavens, and we begin to catch a tiny glimpse of the "so much more" He is doing. He is always working for good in ways we cannot see.

Sometimes my tendency is to look and watch for the big things He might do. But it is in the everyday little things that I catch more of a glimpse of His bigness. This morning I noticed the sun on a corner of the pond. The wind was blowing and the combination of the sunlight and the wind caused the water to look as if it were bursting with diamonds, sparking reflections of delight. When I walk in the woods I notice the way His light dances upon the leaves, ever-changing with different degrees. It's easy to miss this simple beauty. And then there's Ridley, our golden retriever. Watching him roll on his back in the thick grass while his tale wags furiously makes me laugh. He is in pure ecstasy. Simple pleasures are so easy to overlook in the craziness of our daily responsibilities.

Entering into His Presence

I have a four-year-old grandson. When asked to describe him one word immediately pops out: eager. When I go to visit him his face lights up. His eyes grow huge with anticipation. His questions overflow with such rapidity that I can hardly understand him. He's like a runner on the starting block ready to explode. He can't wait to see what I have brought him and he wants to know what games I will play with him. His enthusiasm is contagious.

Simply pulling into his driveway and seeing him run into my outstretched arms fills me with joy.

I want to approach God with this same sense of eagerness. I want to run to His out stretched arms and bask in His presence.

What Will We Find in His Presence?

When entering into His presence we will discover a heavenly Father who knows us intimately, understands us completely, and loves us with a perfect love. He is not a stern principal, a difficult earthly father, a mean coach, a frightening teacher, a cantankerous employer, or any other unpleasant authority figure.

Instead, He is God almighty, creator of the universe and lover of you and me. In fact His love was so great that He sent His only Son Jesus to die on the cross in our place that we might be washed clean of our sins and brought into a relationship with Him that will last throughout all eternity.

In His presence we will find safety, laughter, security, beauty, wisdom, and acceptance for starters. He longs to laugh with us! A laughing God? *Really Susan, aren't you stretching things a bit?* I don't think so. I believe it brings Him great joy when we laugh; after all He created laughter! I suspect many of us are far too serious, too intense. We need to lighten up and to laugh more.

In His presence we will discover a heavenly Father who delights in you and in me (Psalm 35:27b).

WHAT IS GOD SAYING TO YOU AND TO ME?

I delight in you. (Pause and let that soak in for a minute.)

In Me, your human longings will be met by My divine longing for you.

Enter into My presence with eagerness and confidence. Begin to view Me with a new set of lenses—this set of lenses is really lenses of the heart. A heart that is eager to notice Me in the little everyday things, to discover more of Me, and the endless ways I want to bless you and love you. In My presence you will discover hope, a pure hope that will not disappoint.

I will be the one to enable you to enter in to my presence! All you have to do is to ask for My help and I will do it.

At this moment our eyes are like those of a newborn. We see only in part. Our vision is a bit blurry. But we can begin the journey of seeing Him more fully knowing that one day we will see Him face to face in all His glory. The apostle Paul reassures us, "Now we see in a mirror dimly; but then face to face. Now I know in part; then I shall know fully even as I have been fully known. What no eye has seen, nor ear heard, nor the heart of man imagined, what God has prepared for those who love him" (1 Corinthians 13:12 and 1 Corinthians 2:9).

Do you long to enter into His presence? To begin the life long journey of seeing how big He is? To discover that He is the God of so much more than we ever imagined? I do and I hope you do too.

Faith can be risky. Are you willing to be brave enough to trust the God who is bigger than your world?

Open my eyes Lord, I want to see Jesus.

I want to see You in Your magnificence, as I never have. Give me a new set of lenses and every day enable me to awaken with a new focus looking for You and noticing You in ways that I never have before. I want to begin the glorious adventure of discovering how very big You are.

YOU ARE INDEED THE GOD OF SO MUCH MORE

This book is really just the title page of what we will be learning the rest of our lives on earth. The theme of my life is to have my vision of Him enlarged so that daily I might see how much bigger He is than I thought He was yesterday, and that in seeing His greatness I would have a more confident assurance that He loves me, He delights in me, and He will never leave me.

How about you? Will you join me in accepting the following invitation?

You are invited
To put on a new set of lenses
and begin the glorious adventure.

A lifetime journey of getting to know how very big I am.

"I have loved you with an everlasting love; I have drawn you with loving kindness." (Jeremiah 31:3, NIV)

RSVP to
Our heavenly Father God,
Jesus Christ His only Son,
and the Holy Spirit our helper.

Date and Comment

A Time to Reflect:

1. Prayerfully consider your response to this invitation and write out your comment and the date.
2. Begin to expand your vision of how big God is by choosing one character trait of His first thing in the morning to focus on for that day. To get you started see the list in appendix 2. Continue to develop this habit on your own. John 14:26 promises, "The Counselor, the Holy Spirit, whom the Father will send in my name, will teach you all things, and will remind you of everything I have said to you." Ask Him to be your teacher and the one to remind you.
3. Look through your Bible and underline all the places you see "I will" and "I am." As you do this pray:

    "Open my eyes that I might behold wondrous things out of your law" (Psalm 119:18).

Find a friend who will begin this adventure with you and with whom you can share your discoveries of how very big our God is.

Appendix 1 : Finding Certainty

Helpful Hints for Growing in a Relationship with Christ

It's hard to be sure about anything is today's world. After all we have so many questions. But certainty does not preclude questions. We don't have complete understanding. We never will. Much of life is a step of faith. When we step in a car we are not certain we will arrive safely. When we get on the airplane most of us do not have the understanding needed to explain the aerodynamics of how it stays in the air. Simply getting on the plane is a step of faith. Beginning a relationship with God is a step of faith.

One thing is certain—God will not lie. He has promised that if we ask Him to come into our lives, He will. We are likely to have many questions and there will be much we don't understand, especially in the beginning. But, no matter what our background is or what we have done or not done, God longs for each of us to come to Him just as we are. He wants us to have the certainty of knowing Him personally, not simply a vague hope that He exists.

Friend, if you aren't sure that you've ever asked Christ into your life and you would like to, please don't wait any longer. Here is a prayer similar to the one that I and countless others have used to ask Christ to come into our hearts. I encourage you to pray this prayer for yourself and ask Him to come into your heart. We can trust Him to answer questions and to bring understanding as we begin to grow in Him.

Dear Lord Jesus, I need You. I open the door of my heart and ask you to come in. Thank You for dying on the cross for me. Thank You that this painful act of Yours has allowed my sins to be forgiven. Thank You that you have promised that You will never leave me. Thank You that I can know right now that one day I'll be in heaven with You, not because I'm good or bad, but because I'm forgiven.

_____

Your Name and Date

When you ask Christ to come into your heart, several things happen.

1. *He comes in!* You may or may not have experienced strong feelings when you prayed. If you did, that's wonderful. But if you didn't, don't worry. Feelings or lack of feelings don't determine Christ's coming into our lives. He comes in response to being asked. Our relationship with him is not based on our feelings. (What a relief!) It is based on faith in the fact that He will do what He has promised. See Revelation 3:20 and Titus 1:2

2. *He will never leave you.* He promises that even when you forget Him or mess up, He will never leave you. See Hebrews 13:5 and Psalm 139:7-10.

3. *All your sins are forgiven.* When you ask God to forgive your sins, He does. Yes, even that one you can barley admit. He has forgiven that one too. And He stands ready to forgive your future sins when you mess up. All you need to do is to confess them and ask for His forgiveness. See 1 John 1:9 and Psalm 103: 12.

4. *You can know that one day you will be in heaven with Him.* Going to heaven isn't dependent on being good. You could never be good enough. No one can. It is dependent on Christ taking your sins on His shoulders to the cross. See 1 John 5:11-12.

5. *He has given you His Holy Spirit to give you the power to live the life He has planned for you to live.* It isn't up to you to grit your teeth and try harder. Instead, He's given you the full power of the Holy Spirit to enable you to become the person He has created you to be. You can't do it alone. That is not His intention. His intention is that you become more and more dependent upon Him. When you depend on his Holy Spirit, you will experience His supernatural power and freedom. See John 14:26 and 16:13 and Ephesians 1:13-14.

6. *You have a new family of brothers and sisters in Christ who will help you grow in Him.* Just as our children go through different physical growth stages, you

will go through different stages in your spiritual growth. You will need friends you can go to with your spiritual questions. No question, doubt, or feeling is silly or insignificant. You will be helped by having others who have "been there" to guide the way. Seek out a church whose teachings are based on the authority of Scripture and find a small group in which to be involved for encouragement. See 1 John 1:1-4 and 1 Thessalonians 5:11.

No longer do you have to *think* or *hope* or *wonder* if you are a believer. Now you are a *"know so"* believer. You *know so* because Jesus promised He would come into your heart if you asked Him to. And Jesus keeps His promises.

Another thing you can know is that you can approach Him with confidence. The Bible says, "In Him (Jesus) and through faith in Him we may approach God with freedom and confidence" (Ephesians 3:12).

And so dear friend, we can approach God with every fear, concern, and confusion we have in life. Nothing is too silly. Nothing will shock Him. Nothing is too difficult for Him to handle. He longs for us to come to Him and to share our hearts with Him just as we long for our kids to confide in us. He loves us even more than we love our own children, so just imagine how much it thrills Him when we come to Him.

My prayer is that your vision of God will grow and grow and that you will enjoy the journey in discovering to a deeper degree how very much He loves you. Our God is indeed bigger than any of our issues.

Appendix 2: 31 Days of Focus on Our Big God

One of the lessons I continue to learn is how important it is *to focus on who God is rather than on who we are or are not*. It's so easy for our problems, issues, and fears to become larger than our God. There's a wonderful promise in John 14:26 which says that one of the jobs of the Holy Spirit is to be the one who reminds us of all that Christ has taught us. "But the Helper, the Holy Spirit, whom the Father will send in my name, He will teach you all things and bring to your remembrance all that I have said to you." John 14:26

No matter what season of life we are in it is helpful to ask the Holy Spirit to remind us daily of one of God's character traits. Then try to reflect on this trait throughout the day.

I am including 31 days of character traits—one for each day of the month—for you to reflect upon as you journey towards understanding how very big our God is. I hope this will be a place for you to begin and I hope you will develop your own list. I continue to do this in my own daily quiet times. You can sign up on my web site, SusanAlexanderYates.com, to receive two each week in your email.

THANK YOU THAT YOU ARE A GOD WHO...

1. **Rescues...** *You long to rescue me, my relative, my child, my friend. (Psalm 18:19; 91:14-16)*

2. **Delights in me...** *At this moment you are delighting in me, and in ___. (Psalm 35:27b, Zephaniah 3:17)*

3. **Goes before...** *You are going before me and my child to prepare the way. (Ephesians 4:12, Psalm 48:14)*

4. **Is in charge...** *When it seems everything is falling apart I can count on the fact that you are still in charge. (Psalm 75:3; 103:19)*

5. **Lavishes...** *You are lavishing your love on me! (Ephesians 1:8, Ps 145:7)*

6. **Knows all...** *You know everything about me. You know me better than myself and you love me. (Psalm 139)*

7. **Speaks...** *You do speak in your time, in your way. You demonstrate this in creation! (Psalm 25:14)*

8. **Understands...** *When no one else can, you do-completely Oh Lord. (Psalm 139; 147:5)*

9. **Is present...** *Your presence is with me. You never leave me. You are a "with me" God. (Exodus 33:14, Ps 34:18)*

10. **Is light...** *Even if there is darkness around there is no darkness in you. (1 John 1:5, Psalm 27)*

11. **Always forgives...** *Even when I can't forgive myself or others, you do and you enable me to. (Psalm 86:5, 1 John 1:9)*

12. **Creates new things...** *You never get stale. You are always doing something new. (Ephesians 4:24, Ezekiel 36:26)*

13. **Is always working...** *Even when I can't see it, you are working while I'm waiting. (Psalm 103)*

14. **Fills...** *Lord, I'm empty. Please fill me today with your Holy Spirit. (Ephesians 1:23)*

15. **Is exerting power...** *You have the same power that raised a dead man at work in my life, in ____'s life. (Ephesians 1:19-20)*

16. **Holds...** *You are holding your child by your right hand and sustaining her. (Psalm 55:22)*

17. **Covers...** *You are covering me today. You are covering ____. (Psalm 91:4)*

18. **Provides...** *You are providing in ways I don't even know and you will provide in the future. (1 Timothy 6:17)*

19. **Is faithful...** *I can always count on you. You always come through. (1 Corinthians 1:9)*

20. **Is so much more...** *You are so much more and will do so much more than I can imagine. (Ephesians 3:20-21, Hebrews 11:40)*

21. **Delivers...** *You will deliver me, my child, my friend. (Psalm 34)*

22. **Shows unfailing kindness...** *You are caring about my concern at this very moment. (Psalm 18:50; 106:7)*

23. **Is revealing...** *You will reveal your will in your*

time. *(Proverbs 3:5-7, Psalm 90:17)*

24. **Equips...** *You are equipping me for what you have called me to do. (1 Thessalonians 5:24)*

25. **Pours out love...** *Your love isn't parceled out, it's poured out! (Psalm 13:5; 130:7)*

26. **Hears...** *You do hear me – always! (Psalm 31:21-22; 116:1-2)*

27. **Is protecting...** *You are a "watching over me" God! (Psalm 121)*

28. **Is comforting...** *You will supernaturally console ___ today. (2 Corinthians 1:3-5, Psalm 94:19)*

29. **Is advocating...** *You are my lawyer, my defender. (Jeremiah 50:34)*

30. **Brings out to a place of abundance...** *You will refresh your children! (Psalm 66:12b; 31:7-8)*

31. **Is praying...** *Right at this moment you, Jesus, are praying for me, for ___. (Hebrews 7:25, Romans 8:34)*

Chapter 1:

1. J. B. Phillips, *Your God Is Too Small: A Guide for Believers and Skeptics Alike* (New York: Simon & Schuster, 2004).

Chapter 2:

1. For more, read *And Then I Had Teenagers, Encouragement for Parents of Teens and Preteens* by Susan Alexander Yates, and *Barbara and Susan's Guide to the Empty Nest* by Barbara Rainey and Susan Yates.

2. Sarah Young, Jesus Calling, Nashville: Thomas Nelson, 2004, P. 360. Entry for Dec. 9.

3. For more, read *Raising Kids with Character that Lasts* by John and Susan Yates.

4. Ibid.

Chapter 3:

1. John Shifflman, "From abuse to a chat room, a martyr is made—Jane's Jihad." Rueters. http://www.reuters.com/article/us-usa-jihadjane-idUSBRE8B60GP20121207. Accessed: Feb. 16, 2016.

Chapter 5:

1. Thanks to my son John for these thoughts, which he shared with me. He found Ross Douthat's book,

Bad Religion, How We Became a Nation of Heretics to be particularly helpful in discussing this form of idolatry. (New York City: Free Press, 2012). p. 192, 122, 120.

2. Billy Graham, *Just As I Am.* (San Francisco: Harper, 1997). p. 139.

3. Harold Lindsell, *Lindsell Study Bible: The Living Bible Paraphrased.* (Wheaton, IL: Tyndale House, 1971).

Chapter 6:

1. "Juxtapostion." Collins English Dictionary. http://www.collinsdictionary.com/dictionary/english-thesaurus/juxtaposition. Accessed: Feb. 16, 2016.

2. For more, read *And Then I Had Teenagers, Encouragement for Parents of Teens and Preteens* by Susan Alexander Yates and *Barbara and Susan's Guide to the Empty Nest* by Barbara Rainey and Susan Yates.

3. James Finley, *Merton's Palace of Nowhere.* (Notre Dame, IN: Ave Maria Press, 1978). p 114.

Chapter 7:

1. Rabbi Louis Jacobs, "Celibacy" in *The Jewish Religion: A Companion.* (Oxford: Oxford UP, 1995). Online version: http://www.myjewishlearning.com/article/celibacy/. Accessed Feb. 16, 2016.

2. For more, *Read Singles at the Crossroads: A Fresh Perspective on Christian Singleness*, by Al Hsu (Downers Grove, IL.: InterVarsity, 1997) and *Revelations of a Single Woman: Loving the Life I Didn't Expect* by Connally Gilliam (Wheaton, IL: Tyndale House, 2006).

3. Curt Thompson, M.D, *Anatomy of the Soul: Surprising*

Connections between Neuroscience and Spiritual Practices That Can Transform Your Life and Relationships. (Carol Stream, IL, Salt River, 2010) p. 90.

4. Pope John Paul II, *Letter of His Holiness Pope John Paul II to Artists.* (Vatican City: Vatican, 1999).

Chapter 8:

1. Oswald Chambers, *My Utmost for His Highest,* (Uhrich, OH,: Barbour, 2008). Entry for June 21.

Chapter 9:

1. For more, read *Tear Soup: A Recipe for Healing After Loss,* by Pat Schwiebert and Chuck DeKlyen. (Portland, OR: Greif Watch, 1999). A great book for children and adults.

2. Sarah Young, *Jesus Calling,* (Nashville: Thomas Nelson, 2004). Entry for Feb. 21.

3. Dan Allender, *Sabbath.* (Nashville: Thomas Nelson, 2009). p. 161.

Section 3 Overview:

1. "Baby Sensory Development: Sight." Babycenter Expert Advice, http://www.babycenter.com/0_baby-sensory-development-sight_6508.bc. Accessed Feb. 16, 2016.

Chapter 10:

1. Original composer unknown, "His Banner over Me Is Love." https://www.licensingonline.org/en-ca/sku/12702.

ACKNOWLEDGEMENTS

One of the most important things I've learned over the years is the necessity of close friends—friends who will encourage you, confront you, and especially pray for you!

When I first began writing this book I asked God to give me five women who felt called to pray for this particular project. I didn't want to ask anyone. Instead I asked God to chose them and have them approach me. What fun it was to see God send these women to me. When they joined the team they had no idea of the long, arduous journey they were signing up for! They've reassured me when I've almost given up, laughed with me when God has done funny things, hosted lunches for me, sent me encouraging texts and emails when I've struggled, and stood with me for two years. Their fervent prayers have carried me and made all the difference in this book. Thank you Linda Christie, Connie Lindsley, Erin O'Keefe, Judy Stokes, and Carolyn Anderson.

My son John and his wife Alysia read and gave me helpful, honest feedback on the first version as did Melody Ries, my "grace sister!" My friend Lisa Simmons has rescued me many times with her wise insights on content and words. My sister, Fran Cade, always knows just what to say. And my daughter Allison brings uncanny clarity to my decisions.

Other faithful friends have prayed for me and

encouraged me. I am grateful for Molly Shafferman, Barbara Rainey, Elaine Metcalf, Esther Powell, Heidi Little, Ann Holladay, Anne Patterson, Rachel Marotta, Jodie Berndt, Mary Henderson, Judy Thomsen, Jackie Henneberg, Gail Nolan, Christin Stevens, Sarah Klotz, Jessica Blanchard, Amy Hartman and my sister-in-law, Toler Edwards.

A group of young pastors' wives with whom I've met for nine years and love dearly—Jennifer Glade, Mary Ellen Miller, Sarah Kurchina, Jordan Ware, Beth Wall, and Laurel Hanke—are a rich blessing to me. The "Sewickley gang" (Jackie Johnson, Sally Rogers, Nancy Kitch, Sue Henry, Jody Black, Suzonne Smith, Molly Henning, Jennie Lou Amy, and Nancy Courtney) has shared life with me since our kids were toddlers. A group of women with whom I've prayed for our nation's leaders for over twenty years have also prayed for this project. Thank you Eileen Bakke, Kate Giaimo, Janet Hall, Holly Leachman, Joanne Kemp, Linda Slattery, Susan Baker, Carolyn Wolf, Jan Coe, and Grace Nelson.

I am grateful to the women of the Falls Church Anglican, my church family. Many of these women have shared their stories for this book. I have changed some names to preserve their privacy.

Dr. Steve Garber and Dr. Art Lindsley contributed wise theological advice. Jess Oliver, MD. gave clarity to the theme of eyesight. I'm thankful to C J Ausmus, Caleb Burr, and Nate Robbins for their research support.

My agents Robert Wolgemuth and Austin Wilson have been there since the beginning. Thank you guys!

I am grateful to those who have read and endorsed this book. I know not one of you had time to do this and I appreciate you.

My publishing team—Matt and Lisa Jacobson, Gretchen Louise, and Sandra Peoples have brought this project to life. And in the process become dear friends.

Support always comes from my siblings, Syd and Laurie Alexander, Frank and Joan Alexander, and Fran and Catlin Cade.

Our kids, Allison and Will Gaskins, John and Alysia Yates, Chris and Christy Yates, Susy and Scott Anderson, and Libby and McLean Wilson are my *greatest treasurers*, cheerleaders, and prayer warriors.

It is to *your* children, the next generation, that I dedicate this book.

I am trusting the promise of Isaiah 59:21 (which is on the Blessing Bed at the farm!):

"As for me, this is my covenant with them says the Lord, My Spirit who is on you, will not depart from you and my words that I have put in your mouth will always be on your lips, on the lips of your children and on the lips of their descendants from this time on and forever," says the Lord.

To my husband Johnny, my best friend forever. Your faithful early morning prayers for me and our family for over forty-six years is the greatest gift I've ever received. I am so glad I get to live with you!

ABOUT THE AUTHOR

Susan Yates has written thirteen books and speaks both nationally and internationally on the subjects of marriage, parenting, and women's issues. Her books include *And Then I Had Kids: Encouragement for Mothers of Young Children, And Then I Had Teenagers: Encouragement for Parents of Teens and Preteens, Barbara and Susan's Guide to the Empty Nest* (with friend Barbara Rainey) and *Raising Kids with Character That Lasts* (with her husband John).

In addition to writing at her own blog, (SusanAlexanderYates.com) she is a regular contributor to the blog Club31Women. For eleven years she was a regular columnist for *Today's Christian Woman* magazine. She has also written for other publications including *Thriving Family*, a magazine published by Focus on the Family. She's the mother of five children (including a set of twins) all married, and the grandmother of twenty-one (including a set of quadruplets!). Susan and her husband John have been married forty-six years. Together they speak at Family Life's "Weekend to Remember" Marriage Conferences. They live in Falls Church Virginia, a Washington D.C. suburb where John is the senior pastor of The Falls Church Anglican.

But what is she really like? Her blood "bleeds blue." She's a Tarheel, a graduate of the University of North Carolina. She loves Monday night football, ACC basketball, shooting hoops with her grandsons, hiking and riding horseback with her husband, running—especially on country roads, eating chocolate, playing practical jokes on folks, walking and talking with girl friends. You are not likely to find her at the mall; she'd rather be at the farm. You won't find her in the kitchen by choice; she'd rather be outdoors with her golden retriever. Her favorite time of the year is June when all her kids and grandkids are together for a week of "cousins and family camp" in the foothills of the Shenandoah Mountains of Virginia.

To learn more visit:

susanalexanderyates.com

Books by Susan Yates

And Then I Had Kids:
Encouragement for Mothers of Young Children

And Then I had Teenagers:
Encouragement for Parents of Teens and Preteens

Character Matters: Raising Kids with Values that Last
(with John Yates)

Barbara and Susan's Guide to the Empty Nest
(with Barbara Rainey)

How to Like the Ones You Love:
Building Family Friendships for Life

31 Days of Prayer for My Teen (a Parents' Guide)

31 Days of Prayer for My Child
(a Parents' Guide with Allison Yates Gaskins)

Thanks Mom for Everything
(with Allison Yates Gaskins)

Thanks Dad for Everything
(with Allison Yates Gaskins)

Building a Home Full of Grace
(with John Yates)

Marriage: Questions Women Ask
(with Gigi Graham Tchividjian and Gloria Gaither)

Tightening the Knot
(with Allison Yates Gaskins)